Understanding Civilizations

Books by James K. Feibleman

DEATH OF THE GOD IN MEXICO
CHRISTIANITY, COMMUNISM AND THE IDEAL SOCIETY
IN PRAISE OF COMEDY
POSITIVE DEMOCRACY
THE MARGITIST
THE THEORY OF HUMAN CULTURE
THE REVIVAL OF REALISM
AN INTRODUCTION TO PEIRCE'S PHILOSOPHY
JOURNEY TO THE COASTAL MARSH
THE LONG HABIT
AESTHETICS
ONTOLOGY
PHILOSOPHERS LEAD SHELTERED LIVES
TREMBLING PRAIRIE
THE DARK BIFOCALS
THE INSTITUTIONS OF SOCIETY
THE PIOUS SCIENTIST
INSIDE THE GREAT MIRROR
RELIGIOUS PLATONISM
FOUNDATIONS OF EMPIRICISM
BIOSOCIAL FACTORS IN MENTAL ILLNESS
MANKIND BEHAVING
THE TWO-STORY WORLD
MORAL STRATEGY
GREAT APRIL
THE REACH OF POLITICS
THE WAY OF A MAN
THE NEW MATERIALISM
SCIENTIFIC METHOD
THE QUIET REBELLION
UNDERSTANDING PHILOSOPHY
COLLECTED POEMS
THE STAGES OF HUMAN LIFE

Co-Author of

SCIENCE AND THE SPIRIT OF MAN
THE UNLIMITED COMMUNITY
WHAT SCIENCE REALLY MEANS

Understanding Civilizations

The Shape of History

JAMES K. FEIBLEMAN

HORIZON PRESS New York

For Stanley and Judy Feldman

Preface

The lives of most people are lived in and shaped by one of the great civilizations. We of the Western civilization, which covers all of Europe and the Americas, are awakening more and more to the fact that other civilizations are in many respects different from ours and that some of them, the civilizations of ancient India and China, for instance, can boast of achievements of their own.

Just what is civilization and how does it differ from primitive culture? How does a civilization get started, how does it happen to have a life-cycle similar to that of living organisms? More importantly, perhaps, who was the first to advance the *idea* of civilization and how was that idea developed?

For some of the answers to these questions I have gone to the leading authorities of the past and present. What I have found I have tried to present in simple language. Those without special preparation should have no difficulty in reading what I have written. If I have succeeded they should come away from the book with a better grasp of history and a deeper insight into the conditions of our own times.

New Orleans
April 1975

Contents

Understanding
Civilizations

Chapter I

Reading about Civilizations

Other People, Other Ways

When I was in my early twenties I had the opportunity to spend a lot of time in France, chiefly in Paris. By accident I fell in with an international set, and was a party to a few of their goings on. Some of them were rich, some were poor; some were famous, some obscure: a wealthy banker from Hong Kong, a beautiful French actress; in another group, journalists from London, poets from Norway, French writers and painters, and an assortment of adventurers from all over. Most were intelligent, all were sensual, and the conversation was knowledgeable, witty and fast-moving. It was a dizzying experience for a boy who had not often been out of New Orleans, Louisiana.

Later I became friends with a few more typical Frenchmen and their families: small business men, doctors and lawyers. I found them fascinating, too, and very different from the members of the same professions I had known back home.

At night in Paris I happened to come across the novels of Sinclair Lewis which had just been published, especially *Main Street* and *Babbitt*. They were about people in small towns in America. From my life in France it was just like reading about an exotic country I had not visited, a Never-Never-Land of odd customs and traditions. I hardly recognized it.

That was when I first came to understand that although people in broad general terms are very much alike they live in quite different cultures. They may, however, be inter-related. And so there is more, much more, to it than mere acquaintance with people whose ways seem very strange, for we may be involved with them.

I once happened to mention to a garage mechanic while he was repairing my car that I had just heard on the radio that Japan had invaded French Indo-China. That was on September 22, 1940. His comment was, "Well, you know, those people are always fighting". And he added that he did not see what it had to do with him. I did not see what it had, either. But a little more than a year later, December 7, 1941, came Pearl Harbor, and not long after that my mechanic was drafted into the army and sent overseas.

So it did have something to do with him after all. It always does. In the modern world, which is much smaller than it used to be, even though we may not care to be our brother's keeper we must never lose sight of the fact that he may try to be ours. In short, learning something about the forces at work in civilizations may turn out to be a matter of self-preservation.

The fact that we are separated from other people by space and time leads to wide differences in familiarity. Think of the strangeness that would be experienced if a citizen from the interior of China could be exchanged for one from the interior of our country.

Some things, however, do remain the same.

In 1820 John White, in a ship from Salem, Massachusetts, visited Saigon with the avowed purpose of discovering whether trade with Vietnam, particularly in sugar, could be established. (Vietnam in those days was known to the west as Cochin China.) One hundred and fifty years ago he concluded that due to the treacherous and unreliable nature of the government and the people it would not be profitable.

But during his stay he made many observations that interest us now. For instance when he first arrived the Emperor was engaged in putting down a revolt in the northern sections of his kingdom. The similarities and the differences between the Vietnamese and the Americans have not altered appreciably in the last century and a half.

To understand something of the problems we are faced with, a knowledge of other civilizations is necessary. Imagine yourself a citizen of Calcutta or a native of Ethiopia. What would your life be like in a land far away, with quite different customs and traditions, Afghanistan, say, or Mozambique?

That started me thinking about the human condition.

Have you ever wondered why people are so anxious to take their vacations abroad and why they return home so refreshed? It is because they encounter civilizations very different from the one they left behind. This may not be so true of trips to Europe, for after all our ancestors were Europeans and they brought their culture over with them. But a visit to Asia would make a decided difference. I cannot think of anything that would help you to understand your own country better than to take a good look at it from the perspective of a small village in India. You could not understand India in so short a time, but you would understand America much better.

The obvious differences would not be the only ones. You would have to learn a new language which did not much resemble English, and you would be living among people who had the same basic needs as yours but satisfied them in quite different ways. You would be eating food prepared in ways you had not seen before. You would be wearing native clothes that did not look like yours. The customs would not be the same, and the traditions would not, either. You would not have much trouble appreciating the paintings and sculpture that you saw but you would have a lot of trouble with the music.

The best way to learn another language is to live among people who don't speak yours. To get your needs adequately attended to you would have to learn theirs. And if theirs were all you heard day and night, you would soon acquire a familiarity with it if not exactly a mastery over it; at least enough to make it through the day without too much difficulty.

This would be of great benefit to you because you would be at home in at least two cultures. But the greatest benefit still would be the insight it would give you into your own culture, the one you had temporarily left behind. You would be able to look at American customs and traditions, politics and art, and even listen to American music, in a new light and with a depth of understanding you did not know was possible.

You would not realize it, either, but you would have begun the study of civilizations. Many contemporary peoples have lives which are unique. A desert Arab, an African pygmy, a Peruvian mountaineer, a native New Yorker, though basically the same human animal, have little in common, indeed almost nothing they could discuss. It has not been sufficiently recognized that cultural differences go very deep, as deep probably as the organism itself. It would not be hard to accept the truth of this statement if you were to compare the behavior of a New Guinea native with that of a sophisticated Londoner.

We no longer take racial differences seriously, but what about cultural differences? Such differences when summed up become very important because they do as much to keep people apart as race did formerly.

And what about the civilizations of people who lived in earlier times—the classic Greeks, the ancient Egyptians before them, or the Babylonians and Assyrians who were earlier still? What was the shape of the civilizations in which they lived? These are the questions we shall be looking into in the following chapters.

The Alphabet of Civilizations

Most authorities agree that there is one and only one human species. Biologists define a species as a population whose members are capable of interbreeding. From the species point of view, therefore, there is only one "race," the human race; from that point of view, all individuals share a common set of needs. They have to eat and drink, find shelter, make clothing, mate, communicate. For these they need to form societies.

The comparative study of societies has disclosed culture traits common to all of them. Professor G. P. Murdock identified some 76 of these traits, and he insists that all are to be found in every culture known to history. (This applies of course to primitive cultures as well as to high civilizations.) I will name just a few of them: athletic sports, bodily adornment, calendar, cooking, courtship, dancing, division of labor, dream interpretation, education, etiquette, family, folklore, funeral rites, games, gestures, government, greetings, hair styles, housing, joking, language, law, marriage, medicine, music, obstetrics, property rights, puberty customs, religious ritual, sexual restrictions, toilet training, trade, visiting, and weather control.

Murdock's list appeared first in a book edited by Ralph Linton and called *The Science of Man in The World Crisis*, published in 1945. I noted that among the culture traits the last item was some form of weather control. Murdock had said that every culture has one. That was the year I spent Christmas in Sante Fé, New Mexico, and I had gone to the pueblos of the Tusuque Indians on Christmas Eve and again a couple of days later to watch them do their dance for rain.

The following June I found myself in a New York hotel drinking orange juice and reading the *New York Times*, but still thinking about Murdock's culture traits, about weather control and the Tusuque Indians. Clearly, dancing for rain was *their* form of weather control.

But, I thought, the theory is incorrect, for the United States has no form of weather control. And I remembered Mark Twain's joke, that everybody complains about the weather but nobody does anything about it. Then to my amazement my eye fell upon the newspaper page which contained an account of the first attempt to produce rain by seeding clouds with dry ice, which is our form of weather control! Maybe the anthropologists were right after all.

It does not take long to grasp the notion that the human animal is a basic one, with fundamental needs which there are many different ways of satisfying, all of them practiced at one time and place or another. In other words, all of us have some basic similarities over which we have constructed some important differences. We all have the same needs but we provide for them in quite different ways, which depend upon the use of materials, tools and languages.

Material ways of getting things done differ widely and are determined by the stage of development of a civilization. Let me use, as an example, transportation. In a very primitive culture the only way to carry a sick man is on a well man's back. Later stages all involve using vehicles of one kind or another: to pull him in a rickshaw, to carry him in a horse-drawn buggy, to transport him in a train, a motor car, an airplane.

The more complex and sophisticated these tools become the more they have to be made into separate enterprises, with social groups whose special business it is to deal with them. Hence, in addition to the similarity of culture traits, which are in a sense organic, there are undertakings which have become institutional.

Every civilization has such institutions: for example, a government, a system of exchange, a postal service, a family arrangement, schools of some sort, a religion. Often these institutions are so strong that they divide the citizens into social classes: statesmen, wealthy aristocrats, tradesmen, priests, soldiers.

Some institutions are more dominant than others, and the leading institution often runs the country. In the Middle Ages in Europe, for instance, the Roman Catholic Church was the leading institution. In the Soviet Union it is the government. You can tell a lot about what kind of culture it is by which institution has things mostly its own way.

That of course is not the whole story. I have not mentioned the quality of life. Two countries may both value the fine arts but in one country an art may reach a higher peak than in the other. In Germany the production of material goods counts for more than it ever did in Tibet. In the United States the people have much more of a voice in the government. In India, social classes—called castes there—count for more than they do in Brazil.

And I have not yet mentioned the established morality: among every people certain kinds of behavior are prized above others. Manners are important indicators of what people value most; what they value most they seek and expect others to seek with them. Sex is one of the practices which all people indulge in to some extent. But in some civilizations great merit is accorded to those who can do without it, while in others sex is so freely indulged in that there appear to be almost no rules.

Consider the vast differences between societies which value life in *this* world, and societies which place all the emphasis on a supposed life in the *next* world, say that of medieval Christianity. In the middle of either it would be difficult for anyone to bring himself to sympathize with the other.

What holds the members of a society together is a common set of beliefs, customs and traditions. This means that despite the variety of occupations their activities are related in a fundamental way. There is obviously more in common between the English language and English literature than there is between the English language and the Russian language, more between Chinese art and Chinese religion than between Chinese art and American art. Civilizations and even the much smaller primitive cultures operate as independent units.

A man can if he is sensitive to the main currents in his civilization feel himself to be in the middle of a great enterprise, a common effort put together by specialists but no less together for that; the work not only of doctors and lawyers, of politicians and business men, of professors and soldiers, of policemen and ministers, men in different walks of life, all working from the same deeply held convictions and toward common values.

The study of civilizations is the study of the past as well as of the present. I do not mean the study of what we have always called "history," the recital of all that we know of the events which took place at one time and place or another, such events as battles, the deaths of kings, the destruction of cities. I mean rather an account of those larger units of social organization that we have learned to call civilizations; the study of how they are born, how they grow, how they decline and die. Civilizations, though unplanned, are the largest of social or cultural organizations, and they go through life-cycles as human beings do—as anything does, for that matter. To understand the life of a civilization, and to see how one of them follows on another, is something of a new approach.

Another Way to Study History

History is not exactly a new study. All of us have been exposed to it at some point in our education. But there is a new way of looking at history, and that is to view it as the study of civilizations. This approach is not very old and most people are not very familiar with it.

We want to know for instance what there is to know about the achievements of a people which makes us recognize them as composing a civilization, and what is unique about it. Thus armed with a knowledge of similarities and differences, we may pretend to be somewhat acquainted with the species and so to understand something more about history.

In other words, we can look at civilizations the way we can look at anything which came into existence in the world, in two ways: first, how did it get to be what it is—and, second, what is it? The first way is an old one and there are plenty of historians to tell you about it. But the second way has just come to be tried out in comparatively recent times, and has not yet been brought to its full development. The study of civilizations, then, is history looked at in a new way, and it has all sorts of surprising insights and information to offer.

In the effort to trace the outlines of a civilization, you have to forget somewhat the idea of nationality. The two are not the same. Quite a few nations belong to Western Civilization, while the whole of China has been unified in our day for perhaps the first time. Nationalism has been one of the great forces in recent centuries, and when you talk to people you begin to realize that they think in terms of nations. Few recognize Western Civilization, but everyone knows that he is a Frenchman or a Canadian, a Portuguese or an American. Still, nations do form themselves into culture groups which determine the civilizations to which they belong. And though an Englishman may find the idea somewhat distasteful, he has more in common with a Spaniard than he has with a Chinese or an Indian.

The English were the first to make a nation of India, where the languages are not the same for everyone. India is not a nation, of course, but a civilization, a collection of cultures, as a recent traveler put it, each with its own language. The best comparison perhaps would be with Western Civilization with its collection of cultures, too, in this case, French, Spanish, Italian, English, German.

Civilizations do not make advances on every front equally. Each seems to have some special area of achievement in which it excels. Indian Civilization has been religious, Greek Civilization aesthetic, Western Civilization scientific. Such characterization has its limitations, of course. It does not mean that the Greeks knew no science or that the Europeans produced no art.

The Idea of a Civilization

It is the belief of some men, then, that history is not just a chance recital of a sequence of events without rhyme or reason. The past has a shape, and the outlines of that shape can be made out. It takes the form of civilizations which rise and fall. They emerge from previous civilizations, they grow and flourish, they decline and die and finally disappear. That is a comparatively new way of looking at history.

In the western world Greece arose from the ashes of the Minoan Civilization which owed much to the high period of Egypt. Greece was followed by Rome. The Roman Empire gave way to Christian Civilization, which prevailed throughout the Middle Ages. Then the European countries seized the lead, first Italy, then Spain, and after Spain the British Empire. Now, when British power has declined rather sharply and suddenly, the Soviet Union and the United States are quarrelling over the succession. And so it goes.

But what makes it go in that way? What accounts for the rise and fall of civilizations? Thinkers have had different suggestions to explain the facts, and in this book we shall look at some of the more suggestive of these accounts.

Every one of us lives within the confines of some one civilization. As I pointed out earlier, most of us live in what has come to be known as Western Civilization, the civilization that began in Europe and has spread to the United States and other countries. So much is this taken for granted, however, that it hardly seems to be noticed at all, or if noticed then certainly not considered important.

But perhaps it is more important than we think. No civilization lasts forever, and ours is no exception. It comes to this, that you and I are members of a civilization which is only one among many. I invite you to look over my shoulder at what others have thought about civilizations in general, which may help us to understand our own a little better.

Much can be learned from books about other peoples' way of life; much, though surely not all, and perhaps not enough. And yet a reading of what thinkers in other times and places have said about the makeup of civilizations can do something to substitute for personal experience.

There is of course another and perhaps a final point in defense of reading as opposed to travel. It is possible to travel to other places but not to other times. Athens and Rome are still where they were when they were the centers of flourishing civilizations, but they must have looked quite different then. The civilizations that made them great have vanished, and, it is said, even the environment is not the same. The climate has changed and the hills are no longer as wooded as they once were. A Greek from the fifth century B.C. would recognize little in his country if he were to come back to it now, and a Roman would be more than puzzled by what he saw. Rome was destroyed in the fourth century by invading German tribes. The Rome you visit has been rebuilt and reoccupied, and the traffic problems that currently plague the city would convince a Roman from the Augustan Age that he had made a mistake in thinking that it was the place where he had once lived.

What is left of Greece and Rome now is a random collection of ruined buildings partially restored; of artifacts of one kind or another, vases, busts and coins displayed in museums around the world; and above all of translations into many languages of the Greek and Roman classics of literature, history and philosophy, of poetry and drama and epic. All are worth experiencing, but if you do not have some general picture in mind you will be left with a fragmentary impression of precious relics, and that is all.

There have been many great civilizations in the world at one time or another, and they did rise and flourish, decline and die, and they were replaced by others that came after them. I have tried to tell something of that story in this book, using as my choicest examples the best that has been thought and written on the subject.

Chapter 2
The Coming of Civilizations

Before the Coming of Man

I must begin the account of civilizations by reminding you that the universe, even the earth, is much older than man. History is, quite simply, what happened in the world, and there have been an awful lot of happenings for a very long time. To complicate things, we do not always know what happened, and so we have the additional problem that written history is not always the same as history.

Man is a product of his environment, and in a broad sense his environment is the universe—all of it, more than a billion galaxies, each with an average of a billion stars like our sun, and with planets revolving around many of the stars, in a universe which has lasted some 13 billion years.

In other words, there are many places where life could have existed before it began to exist here. The spatial world has afforded a richness of opportunity for life of all sorts to flourish, including animal types more primitive than man but perhaps also others less primitive. Uncounted eons have gone by during which it could have been said of the human species that it had not evolved and of the earth that there was none.

Then came the billions of years of planets; approximately five billions for the earth. The formation there of chemical compounds may have been the result of electrical discharges in gases from early volcanoes. Slowly, organic life developed, by accident, as it were, about four billion years ago; at first, only compounds of acid and protein; but later the most primitive of single-celled organisms. Why physical events in planetary dust and gas should have led to biological organisms is not well understood.

For as long as a billion years there were only algae and sponges. Several hundred million years were required to move from fishes, to coral, to conifers, to mammals, by means of a biology based on a chemical reaction involving the synthesis by green plants of organic compounds from carbon dioxide and water, with sunlight as energy; and a reverse process involving the absorption of oxygen and the emission of carbon dioxide by animals. Some twenty-five million more years of this just to get to creatures with spinal columns.

Plants are stationary and have a strong grip on the earth. The roots of alfalfa plants have been known to penetrate twenty-five feet or more below the surface. But animals are mobile, and especially man: mobile and restless. The animal, man, derived his nature from other animals, from plants, and ultimately from rock erosion and organic debris. Since man as an animal emerged from the environment as a product of it, there can be no reliable knowledge of anything in man that was not first in the environment.

Although some doubt still exists as to his origins, evidence seems to be accumulating that the apes who lived some twenty-five million years ago may have been his true ancestors. The enormous stretches of prehistory are so long that they defy the imagination. And yet, as Jacquetta Hawkes observes, "irreversible events took place during those uncalendared ages. They did much to determine the pattern of the ancient civilizations, and they affect us still."

Some two to three million years ago man-like animals branched off from the monkeys. A number of types can be recognized, chiefly from fossil skulls, as having some of the characteristics of both, but some which leaned toward the human. These have been identified as the ancestors of man, and they have been given the names of the places where they were found. Something of their features can be deduced from reconstructions. They must have been short and strong, with half-simian faces.

Human Beginnings

It was a long but a sure descent from the man-like apes to the ape-like man. But looking back we can see that they were slowly trending in the human direction.

There have been times in the world's history when it was warmer everywhere than it is now. And there have been ice ages. Periodically ice-sheets advanced from the two poles until they covered one third of the earth's surface. Then they retreated to the tenth of that surface which they occupy. There have been three such glacial periods in the last million years. The whole of human civilization has fallen within the early years of the end of such a glacial period.

The earliest human types are dated no more than half a million years ago. The Australopithicines and the Pithecanthropines, some million years older, were closer to man than they were to the apes. Evolution works with incredible slowness, the development which can be described in a single sentence took millions of years. The oldest remains date back for several million. The most primitive types bear only a superficial resemblance to man as we know him, though they most surely were related.

Neanderthal man was hardly what we should call human today but he was capable of shaping stone, and that makes us count him among the true hominids. What distinguished the early types was their upright stance. It led to the greater importance of sight over smell. The last of these man-like creatures, the Neanderthalers, were everywhere in Europe and western Asia. They were not tall but they were large and very powerful, with heavy jaws, large teeth and generally thick limbs.

Some 50,000 to 40,000 years ago they suddenly disappeared, leaving the field to *Homo sapiens*, who has been in charge ever since. This is the species of man as we know him today. Neanderthal man used hand-axes. Is it possible that *Homo sapiens* won because he learned how to make chipped blades?

The authorities tell us that man as he is today has existed for no more than 40,000 years. That is only a moment compared to the vast ages that preceded him. It does make him look like a mere Johnny-come-lately, one of nature's experiments which may succeed or may fail; it is too early yet to say.

Three features of early man can be made out. First, there were few of him. Secondly, he was a nomad. And thirdly, he was a tool-maker. Let us look briefly at each of these.

The early primitive populations of the human species were probably sparse, in the beginning no more than a few families banded together here and there, chiefly for protection against stronger and larger wild animals. Degree of cultural advance seems to be tied to size of population, for until a division of labor appears there can be no specialization and hence no serious progress, and a division of labor is never possible until there are enough men to call on.

Early man was a hunter, and a nomad, for he had to follow the herds of animals upon which he lived. In this connection it might be added that he was a cannibal. He hunted and ate his fellow creatures. Many relics include long bones which have been split like those of wild animals to extract the marrow, and skulls which have been enlarged at the base in order to extract the brain.

Man the animal cannot be separated from his environment. His community is not only his social group but also his material culture. It is almost commonplace now to define man as a tool-maker. From the earliest specimens it is clear that man always has depended on tools for survival. Culture began in fact when the first ape grew weary of climbing and stood erect on the ground in order to free the use of his hands.

In July 1963 in Australia, a rancher on horseback followed by his dog came across a herd of kangaroo feeding. The dog frightened them and they fled, but the dominant male came over and pulled the man off his horse. They were struggling together on the ground, with the fight going against the man, when they rolled into a small stream filled with large stones. The man picked up a stone and with it crushed the skull of the kangaroo and the fight was over. Thus in 1963 the drama of man's device for winning the battle over naturally superior forces in his environment was repeated in the same primitive form in which it no doubt had occurred for the first time a million years earlier.

The Stone Age

In terms of the coming wealth of civilizations, the feature most significant in early man is the one I have already mentioned: his use of tools. The principal advances were made in terms of them. Probably the stone pebble used as a weapon and then the stone axe were first. Then came flint blades, scrapers, the points of projectiles, the graving-tool or burin, calling for more skills and hence for more thought. The chopper-tool and the hand-axe played their part in the development of the human brain. The more complex the stone tools the more complex the tasks it was called on to perform, and the more complex the tasks the more complex the behavior which his brain was obliged to direct.

Of course tools and their uses are both conditioned by the materials available. Men of the Stone Age worked chiefly in stone but also in wood, bone and ivory. Much could be done with these but no more. The materials available always make certain new developments possible.

One of the most useful tools ever invented (though we don't

ordinarily think of it in that way) was the shaping of sounds to convey meanings. Speech, employed at first perhaps only to express emotional states, must have been thought of in order to make cooperation possible in the hunting of large animals which were too powerful for individuals working alone to bring down.

It is difficult to imagine how tools could have been made and passed on without the use of language. Early man probably had some sort of spoken language, though nothing of this has survived. Many thousands of years later than the period we have been describing he still had nothing that could be called a language, only pictures to serve as signs.

It was by means of tools that the Stone Age much later spread out in many directions. The drawings of men and animals on the walls of caves indicate man's growing awareness both of himself and of his environment, while the stone burial mounds, the megaliths of western Europe, testify to his increased technical mastery.

To satisfy his needs he had to reach out into the environment for those materials which contained what he required. But, unlike the other animals, once satisfied he could foresee that the needs would occur again, and so he learned how to plan to meet them in the future. For this purpose it was necessary to cooperate with his fellows in the making and using of particular tools, many of which required a group effort. In this way a continued food and water supply as well as the many other things he needed, such as knowledge and security, were assured.

How did civilization get started? For many thousands of years man had been a nomadic hunter. That is to say, he had followed the herds of animals upon which he lived. It was the only way he knew to insure a plentiful food supply, but it was a way of life involving continual movement, and he could not carry very much in the way of artifacts. Culture had to remain primitive.

Those unknown culture heroes who discovered the use of fire and invented the wheel had a companion whose work may have been of even more importance than theirs. For one day a genius arose who saw that the herds of reindeer and other animals could be fenced in, bred and consumed at will, provided also that crops to feed them were cultivated. A safe date for the earliest farming settlements, for stock-raising and cereal-growing, would be no earlier than 10,000 B.C.

This was the beginning of animal husbandry and agriculture; it was the beginning also of much more. It was in fact what led to civilization as we know it. For with a settled life, more permanent houses could be built, many other artifacts produced, and the whole collection passed on through children to successive generations. This was the village culture of the Stone Age.

Recently anthropologists and others have studied the Kung, a Stone Age people who have been hunters and gatherers for 11,000 years in more or less the same part of the Kalahari Desert in South Africa, and who are now just changing from their nomadic existence to a settled life in villages. The change is having a profound effect on them. The women are no longer considered the equals of men, the children are no longer raised to be non-aggressive, and the size of the population, which had been steady, is rapidly increasing. They are heavier and on the whole less healthy.

The step from hunting to animal husbandry and agriculture was a decisive one so far as human history is concerned. From the nomadic life of the hunter to the settled life of the farmer meant a change of conditions that went as deep as the organism itself. In addition to the feelings of the present there were now plans for the future. The settled life eventually led to the arts of civilization and hence to modern man as we know him.

We cannot follow in detail the connection between the development of the human brain and the use of tools and languages, although no doubt there has been a steady influence. As Alex Comfort has pointed out, it is only a hundred generations or so from the man who hunted boar with a spear to the modern production of beef. Earlier human types had smaller brains, but

250,000 years ago there were already creatures with brains as large as ours. Men have not altered appreciably in the last 40,000 years.

Certainly it is true that the capacity of the brain to acquire vast amounts of information and retain it, to think and plan abstractly, is one of the essential factors in making civilization possible. At some point in man's history this capacity evolved and accelerated to its present capabilities. When we consider how comparatively recent even the first civilizations were we get some idea that the development must have been a sudden one. If man made himself in that sense, surely he was unaware of it at the time and has left no records that we know of.

The Bronze Age

We have been talking chiefly about conditions in the half million years of the Stone Age. It is almost unreasonable to have expected man, who had been accustomed to the roving life of the hunter for some 30,000 years, to adjust himself suddenly to the constricted life of the city. But that is exactly what did happen.

There was an intermediate stage, of course. There had been settled communities of a crude sort for ten thousand years or longer, but little is known about them. It was not until some six thousand years ago that the Bronze Age began, probably with cities in what is now southern Iraq, particularly Sumer. The Sumerian Civilization if not the oldest is one of the oldest. It dates from somewhere between 3500 and 3000 B.C., though it was not until about 2800 B.C. that it came to its full development, which included the earliest known writing.

Not long after that there were civilizations in Egypt on the banks of the Nile and in Mesopotamia on the banks of the Tigris and Euphrates Rivers. There were similar developments in Asia. In what is now Pakistan the Harappá Civilization was based on the great metropolitan centers of Mohenjo Daro on the west bank of the lower Indus River, and Harappá itself on the east bank of the Ravi, and in northern China on the banks of the Yellow River there was the Shang Civilization; we know less about these last two. The Civilization of Dilmun along the Persian Gulf coast and islands from Kuwait to Bahrain seems to have been as old as any, and the Ubaid Culture perhaps even older. In the third millenium B.C. they must have made a continuous chain of civilizations running all the way from Sumer to ancient India.

Sir Leonard Woolley has pointed out that the cities which grew up in the Bronze Age were quite different from the towns of the Stone Age in having a number of citizens not engaged in farming or fishing but instead making up classes of rulers, officials, clergy, artisans and merchants. The division of labor had arrived.

It was a great day when men learned how to mix tin with copper to form bronze. Civilization, we may say, began as a result of the discovery of bronze. Human progress consists of many developments, but by common agreement it can be measured by the given stage of technology, by the complexity of the methods by which men learned to make the things they wanted. Metallurgical techniques have long been the most important; the effects of the discovery of copper and of the process tin to make bronze were startling. Introduced into eastern Europe in 1900 B.C., within a century there was a fully developed culture based upon the manufacture and use of bronze tools and implements. However, the Bronze Age was based not only on the use of a new metal but also on what Gordon Childe has named the Urban Revolution. It occurred for the first time as a product of cities. Stone Age man had for the most part to adapt himself to his environment but by the Bronze Age he was beginning to learn how to adapt the environment to himself.

People do not live in a vacuum. They are hooked up to their environment by the very fact that they need so many of the things which are found in it. When they interact with the environment they alter it but to some extent they also alter themselves. The techniques and the tools which result from their efforts collectively add up to a fundamental change all round. Childe has pointed to some of the inventions which made civilization possible: artificial irrigation, the harnessing of animals to wheeled vehicles, the sailboat, the use of copper and the making of bricks, a solar calendar and writing.

With every technological advance, larger concentrations of population became possible. More efficient communication and transportation of course played essential roles. Consider what happened to transportation, for instance. In the later Stone Age there were crude wagon wheels of clay. By the Bronze Age there were horse-drawn vehicles.

What we are witnessing is an increase of differences among cultures. Stone Age practices tended to be everywhere alike, but this was not the case with the Bronze Age. The best example comes from the Shang Civilization, roughly from 1700 B.C. to 1122 B.C. The Chinese of that period already believed in the importance of death, for the spirits of ancestors had power over their living descendents and thus became not only sources of guidance but also objects of worship. No other Bronze Age peoples had such a custom so intensely and none practiced it for so long.

There is no doubt of the vast importance that religions have played in the development and continuance of civilizations. But the existence of civilizations is one thing, and the awareness of civilizations is quite another. The awareness of civilizations begins when people no longer dismiss their past by attributing it to a divine origin and when they recognize their past as different from those of other peoples.

The motive force for building civilizations is the desire for permanence. Civilizations are born from man's need for security; in order to procure immediate security in this world he needs surplus food supplies, shelters and weapons; for guarantees of ultimate security in the next world he needs ritual burial, temples to gods and monuments to god-kings.

It was probably a haphazard development that groups of

villages spread out until together they formed one large city, and that the city dwellers got separated from the food-producers, a process that probably took roughly a thousand years. The population pressure in the city compelled the discovery of more and more efficient ways of doing things; men became professional artisans, tradesmen, soldiers, administrators while the food-producers became peasants engaged exclusively in crop-raising and stock-breeding.

It is doubtful whether people in ancient Sumeria or Egypt thought of themselves as living in a civilization; indeed it was to be a long time before anyone did. Civilization was the productive alteration of the environment in many different ways by a relatively large population as a great cooperative enterprise. However, there was one difficulty. The men who accomplished these tasks were the descendants of nomads, and they were not able to break away from the accumulated aggression acquired in thousands, perhaps hundreds of thousands of years of nomadic hunting. It is well known from recent experiments that when ordinarily peaceable animals living in the wild are captured and confined in a relatively small space, they begin to fight among themselves.

The nomad lives chiefly by means of his muscles; and although civilized man operates chiefly through the use of his brains, the muscles are of course still there and make their demands, satisfied only by exertion and effort. But the demands of the muscles are not entirely reduced by such constructive work as the making of tools out of raw materials, and there is a process which operates much faster: destruction. The need for activity if carried far enough would explain the frequency of conflicts in civilization and may even account for wars. It has taken a few hundred years to build a great city, but only a few hours to burn one down.

The increase in material culture was as thoroughgoing as it was sudden. The construction of material things on a large scale has proved immensely effective. It has been called man's "ar-

tificial second nature" and in the last few decades it has expanded enormously. By now there is not much in his nearby environment he has not greatly altered. He has cut down the forests,
built cities and farms in the clearings, brought oil and minerals
to the surface, and filled the air with smoke and dust.

The oceans are perhaps the least affected by human activity,
but even they are not entirely free. Travel on the surface of the
sea, submarine exploration, and the dumping of waste products,
are some of the ways in which the oceans, too, are affected. Man
lives in a world of his own making, on terms which he himself
has largely laid down.

Material advances always signal the coming of advanced
ways of thought. By the end of the Bronze Age about 1250 B.C.
writing had been invented, the basic principles of architecture
had been discovered, men had learned how to dye materials,
what to dose a fever with, how to calculate the area of a field,
the cost, in materials, labor and time, of a building. In the
Bronze Age there were many of the evidences of civilizations.
There were walls around Mohenjo-daro, around the city of
Shang in northern China, and in the Middle East around many
of the Hittite cities. There was international trade between all
the great centers of western Asia and there was traffic in the
ideas that often went with it; there were farmers, craftsmen,
rulers, soldiers, aristocrats, citizens, slaves, in a word all the essential inequality of classes. There were codes of law and established religions.

The making of religion is always conditioned by the life of a
people and by their environment. Religions tended at first to be
the products of an immediate neighborhood. The gods of place
might be a sacred wood or a holy stone. The lonely Bedouin in
the desert was likely to have a different kind of religion from the
men in the land of Sumer and Akkad who inhabited cities.

Childe was convinced that the first unifying social forces were
brought into existence by the triumph of one religion over
others. Certainly it is true that the earliest records kept in pic-

torial writing (ideograms) on clay tablets in Sumer and on slivers of wood in Egypt, bear the accounts of temple wealth; both are dated to some 5,000 years ago. The priests were members of large continuing corporations, which may have been the earliest institutions. Certainly the greatest architectural efforts went into the construction of magnificent tombs, which stand as the most concerted effort in those early civilizations. Witness the Pyramids in Egypt and, much later, the Taj Mahal in India.

The development of the population centers and the advances in many departments of culture, made possible by the new knowledge of how to make and use bronze, went so rapidly that by the end of the 13th century B.C. most of the possibilities opened up by the new technology had been explored and exhausted. Not much more could be done in that direction; mankind was ready for the next step.

The Stone Age lasted for hundreds of thousands of years, the Bronze Age survived for only a few thousand before it was superseded. The pace is clearly quickening.

The Iron Age

In the civilizations that existed early in the Bronze Age, a great advance was made with the discovery of each new metal. Iron, and particularly steel, brought with it an increased power. There were taboos against iron in the Old Testament, but it was already in use with the Hittites, who for the two centuries after 1500 B.C. also maintained a monopoly of the trade in steel. The technique of repeatedly plunging iron into cold water after hammering and heating it to give it a hardness superior to bronze was first discovered by the inhabitants of the mountains of Armenia, but the knowledge spread slowly. For Europe it would be proper to say that 1200 B.C. would be the earliest date for the beginning of the Iron Age.

By 800 B.C. iron had reached the Mediterranean world, though the use of bronze was still more common. Homer's heroes fought chiefly with bronze weapons, but Achilles offered prizes of iron. In the high period of Greek culture in the fifth century B.C. the blacksmiths were foreigners; but the father of Sophocles, the dramatist, was a blacksmith, and Demosthenes, the orator, inherited a sword factory. By Roman times both iron and steel had come into general use, so that their manufacture was a recognized profession and large-scale operations were quite common.

In the Iron Age civilizations were beginning to grow markedly. Capital cities were extending their sway over others less powerful, and empires were emerging which included vastly more people and a much greater territory than they did in the Bronze Age. The Persian Empire at its height extended all the way from Bulgaria in the west to the northern part of India in the east, and could boast of a very sophisticated culture, though in that respect it was somewhat dwarfed by the achievements of its tiny and unconquerable neighbor, Greece. When the Emperor Hadrian came to power the Roman Empire stretched over some two million square miles and had a population of more than sixty million.

With the use of iron tools, stones could be shaped with greater precision and so architecture became more advanced. Weapons were made more lethal and armies more efficient, and so conquests could be consolidated. Governments were becoming more highly organized and so could be more effective. Large bureaucracies made their appearance, writing took on a greater significance, men were aware of other civilizations and this made them more self-conscious about their own. They were beginning to think of themselves as members of broad cultures and of following a way of life not shared by others. The Greeks and the Romans travelled and wrote accounts of other civilizations which they recognized to be in many respects quite different. Despite that fact, no study of comparative civilizations was undertaken for many centuries. So far as our records go, advanced studies of civilizations simply did not exist. Only in the last few centuries have such studies had a sudden development.

It would be fair to say that the Iron Age overlapped with its successor, which may be called the Age of Science. The Iron Age reached its highest point in the nineteenth century with large constructions, such as bridges and skyscrapers, which had not been possible before. Fast communication and transportation —for instance the telegraph, railroads, freighters and passenger liners, street cars and automobiles—all owed their invention and manufacture to the discovery of iron and steel.

The Age of Science

It might be called the Age of Aluminum and Magnesium or the Age of Plastics or perhaps better still the Age of Light Tensile Metals, but The Age of Science is more comprehensive. The light tensile metals and the plastics have made possible a great advance, but the advance is not confined to them; it is a product of the discovery of the method of discovery.

Probably we should date the end of the Iron Age and the beginning of the Age of Science from the seventeenth century, a bare three hundred years ago. I pointed out earlier that the pace of civilization has accelerated sharply. This time it was made possible by the discovery of new and more adaptable metals and also by the discovery of new physical and chemical discoveries but chiefly by the discovery of the scientific method whereby further discoveries can actually be provided for and even planned.

Science, as I hope to show shortly, is more than a very new kind of tool-making, though it is that too. The Scientific Revolution is as dramatic a development as the Urban Revolution that started civilization in the first place. It is, in the opinion of many, only the second revolution of such dimensions in the history of mankind. It includes the many kinds of manufactured ar-

ticles—everything from shoes to ships, from bicycles to buildings
—to which we have given the name of material culture. Artifacts, materials altered by men for their own uses, are to be
found everywhere you turn. The extent of the artificial environment has not yet been carefully estimated; no one knows what
effect it will have on man in the long run.

(I exclude here consideration of the problem of pollution of
the environment; solved or not, it is part of the process of turning a natural environment into an artificial one.)

There has been no marked change in man since the events
which brought him to his present condition; no change, that is,
in his biological characteristics. However, it must be remembered as we said, that he is a product of interaction with his environment, and there has been a change in the environment, so
sharp, in fact, that it is too early to say how lasting its effects will
be. But since it is taking individual man with it, the question is
important for him. The increase in material culture is already
very rapid. Within the last 6,000 years, and more particularly
within the last few hundred, man has invented an environment
which is almost altogether artificial, with the consequence that
he now lives in a world which is to a large extent one of his own
constructing. By adapting to this artificial environment, he has
improved himself—at least up to a point. And if that point was
reached some 40,000 years ago and there has been no biological
improvement since that date, it may be because the period is too
short for evolutionary changes to occur. But it may be also
because biological improvement has been replaced by improvement in material culture. Biological inheritance is transmitted
from parents to children, whereas the inheritance of material
culture is transmitted to an entire contemporary generation, obviously a great gain in efficiency. What the men and women
pass on to children in addition to the biological inheritance is a
complex, stress-producing material culture—in a word, a civilization.

(The building of a special environment by industrial man has led some authorities to suppose that he has been set free. The truth would appear to be quite the opposite, for he is more tightly tied in to his environment now than he was before. Primitive man always did live in a world containing some artificial things, but civilized man lives in a world composed almost entirely of them. The things he is chiefly concerned with are those he has altered to suit his own purposes. Very little around him is as it was before he made his alterations in it; certainly not the earth on which he stands nor the air he breathes.

Thus now he can exist only in a modern civilization. He has adapted to its requirements so completely that he would be unprepared to meet any other kind. The clock cannot be turned back. Those primitive cultures which still exist in remote corners, such as the mountainous interior of New Guinea or the desert of central Africa, cannot hope to survive in the long run without coming to terms with civilization in one way or another. In many cases without the increased productivity that science and technology have made possible for agriculture, whole populations would starve. What this will do to the human species eventually it is too soon to say. Evolution is a slow process even at its most rapid and the latest developments are too new to evaluate.

The earliest history of man includes an account of his tools and languages. Yet the fact that without man there would be neither tools nor languages has perhaps blinded us to the further fact that without tools and languages there would be no man— certainly not man as we know him. It is the articles he has made out of the materials at hand which have enabled him to develop his upright posture, unusual skills, brains, trades, institutions, entire civilizations.

Civilization Arrives

Civilization represents the efforts of man to continue the existence of his species. For he is culture-bound. He does not live in a world by himself but in the civilization his ancestors have made and which he and his contemporaries have inherited and modified.

Civilization in a word is the rearrangement by man of his environment. The Scientific Revolution has placed in his hands not only the mastery of the whole earth but also the technology to reach beyond it. Other planets beckon to him and, as we shall see in a last chapter, perhaps even other solar systems.

If man has a leading principle it is this: he is the animal which tries to exceed itself. Every mark he has left upon his genes in the successive stages of his evolution, every scratch upon every stone which has survived, offers evidence of the truth of this principle. He does not act merely in the interest of satisfying his needs but reaches out beyond them to make contact with the rest of the cosmic universe through thought (for instance by means of philosophical systems), through feeling (the claims of supernatural revelations) and through action (the exploration of space).

The chief lesson of prehistory is that man makes his own arrangements with his environment partly in terms of his inherited nature but also partly in terms dictated by the conditions he finds there. Matter is stubborn, as we have always known; it is also complex, as we have learned only recently; much can be done with it when it is properly understood. Our complex machines and our enormous controls over nature are the results of this understanding. Man emerged from a natural background and belongs in it no less now than when his ancestors hid in caves and forests which they hardly disturbed by their presence. The study of human nature must take this inheritance into account.

Civilized man is the result of efforts to meet the demands of the city. It is in the city where so many of his responses have been made constructively that he has learned to do by means of manufactured articles what formerly he had done only with his body and in a crude and primitive way. Perhaps it is not too much to say that the measure of a civilization is the extent to which the functions of the human body can be transferred to machines. The motor car and the airplane carry him farther and faster than his legs, libraries are larger and more retentive than memory, stoves are better than stomachs at breaking down vegetable fibers.

In a word, civilization is city-ization. Everything that we cherish most has come out of the city, the plays of Shakespeare, the music of Bach, the paintings of Velasquez, the knowledge of the law of gravitation of Newton, the theory of evolution of Darwin, even things for rural use, such as chemicals for increasing the yield of wheat and drugs for treating cattle.

What then is a civilization? Let me restate it in a little more detail. A vast but loose organization of established ways of meeting needs which have become customary and traditional and which involve material tools and some planning by a settled community. All the distinctive features of a culture, its population, its means of livelihood, its technology, economy and social organization, are bonded together.

In the six thousand years of civilizations that lie behind us there have not been so many different ones; at the most a couple of dozen. No wonder then that we are new to their study. In the following chapters we shall look at some of the accounts of them which have been presented by leading thinkers.

Chapter 3
Early Accounts of Civilization

The earliest accounts of the succession of civilizations that we have are contained in the Book of Daniel in the Bible, and in the work of Hesiod in ancient Greece. The civilization of the ancient Hebrews is as old as any, and probably can be dated back before 1800 B.C., with its origins in or near Sumeria, but the Old Testament was not written down much before the sixth century B.C.

Of all the ancient civilizations which are known to have existed, none has left us any records of a theory of history. Did anyone in Assyria, in Babylonia or in the Indus Valley, entertain such ideas? Possibly; but we have no way of knowing; we shall have to confine our attention to the later records we do have. Writing is highly perishable, and the remains of most of the ancient civilizations do not include very much in the way of writing. Civilizations, then, but no *accounts* of *comparative* civilizations.

The accounts given by Daniel and Hesiod are exceedingly brief, less than a page apiece, and very sketchy, but at least they show that men were thinking about the problem. They marked the first steps in the recognition by a people that it had a history and even took the second step in recognizing that its history had a shape. How much of them was made up of fact and how much of folk-tale it is not difficult to see. As you will note from the stories themselves, they recite events which could never have happened, but they may contain symbolically the substance of some important beliefs, for the form of myth often holds essential truths, the result of centuries of tradition.

Daniel's Four Ages

That the Jews had an account of history beginning with a golden age of their own as early as the earliest dates for the Old Testament, is attested by the story in *Genesis* of the Garden of Eden, where conditions were idyllic and there was pleasure and no pain. It was short-lived. Though painfully brief and given in allegorical terms, it still may be mentioned as making a beginning.

Daniel was evidently an historical person who seems to have lived from 606 to 535 B.C., though nothing is known about him. In the Book of Daniel, chapter 7, are to be found the materials of a dream, Daniel's vision of four beasts which emerged from the sea: a lion with eagle's wings, a bear with three ribs in its mouth, a leopard with four wings and four heads, and a terrible beast with ten horns. Then God sitting on his throne judged the beasts: the fourth one was killed and burned, the others lost their dominion but lived on for a time. Then "one like unto a son of man" arrived with the clouds of heaven and received everlasting dominion.

An angel, who just happened to be standing next to Daniel, explained to him the meaning of his dream. The beasts were the four kingdoms of the Chaldeans, the Medes, the Persians, and the Seleucids (The Hellenistic Empire), respectively. After them the kingdom would pass to the Jews.

In chapter 7 at line 27, there is the promise of an everlasting kingdom for the faithful. But in chapter 12 there is forecast the coming of "a time of trouble such as never was since there was a nation" for the others, when the dead shall arise from their graves and there shall be a Last Judgment.

This account is *not* enough to amount to a cyclical theory of history, but it is at least a theory of history, however crude and mythical. There is just a suggestion of repetition, but hardly enough to go on. The honor of initiating a cyclical theory must go to the Greeks. The first name that occurs in this connection is that of Hesiod, and the second that of Plato.

Hesiod's Five Ages

Greek Civilization is now thought to have lasted longer than was formerly supposed. It was begun in Mycenae in the southern part of what is now mainland Greece, probably about 1400 B.C. It ended abruptly 200 years later, and then there is a gap of 400 years before the culture which we now know as Greek appeared. It was based on Athens and other cities on the mainland but also on the coast of Asia Minor and in the Aegean Islands.

The Greeks, chiefly the Athenians, invented everything that was later taken up in the Western Civilization of Europe and the Americas except representative democracy (they had direct democracy), polyphonic music (they had monophonic), and experimental science (which they had, too, but did not develop). In addition they also suffered deception, treachery and civil war, and so their achievements were short-lived.

The Greeks had historians, of course, and great ones, such as Herodotus and Thucydides. But only two Greek thinkers have left us any record of a cyclical theory of history. This was the work of Hesiod in the archaic early period and of Plato in Greece at its height.

Hesiod's dates are uncertain but they seem to have been about the eighth century B.C. Hesiod's father was a refugee from Asia Minor. Like his father, Hesiod was a Boeotian farmer, settled in Ascra, a village near Helicon, in northern Greece, "bad in winter, wretched in summer, good at no time." He was a shepherd and he learned songs as he was tending lambs under Mount Helicon. In his work he was given to so many rustic expressions that we can well believe him. Many of them are charming: the snail is a "house-carrier," the snake is "the hairless one" and the burglar is "the day sleeper." Later on he seems to have made his living, like Homer, as a wandering singer, and according to his own account, he was the winner in a song contest held in Chalcis in Euboea. The prize was a tripod, which he dedicated to the Muses of Mount Helicon. Eventually he retired to Locris, where Plutarch says he was entertained by two brothers, who murdered him when they suspected him of seducing their sister.

Of his two chief works, the *Theogony* and the *Works and Days*, the former, an account of the Greek gods, is one he may have organized rather than written, and he seems to have regarded it as an introduction to a universal history. That history itself is contained in *Works and Days*.

It begins oddly enough with a story which will remind my readers of Adam and Eve and the Garden of Eden. In Hesiod's account they are known as Epimetheus and Pandora. (The name, Pandora, translates as "all-endowed.") Because Iapetus had stolen fire from heaven against the express command of Zeus, the father of all the gods, Zeus ordered Hephaestus to mix earth with water and to make a beautiful maiden. With the help of many of the other gods she was taught all the arts of womankind. "Golden Aphrodite shed grace upon her head and cruel longing" and Hermes "put in her a shameless mind and a deceitful nature." She was garlanded with necklaces of gold and crowned with flowers. She was called Pandora and sent to Epimetheus as a gift. His brother Prometheus had warned him never to accept a gift from Zeus but "to send it back for fear it might be harmful to men." But he took the gift and "when the evil thing was already his he understood." There was a jar containing the other gifts of the gods. When Pandora took off the lid all sorts of evil flew out, countless plagues and diseases and mischief of all sorts.

According to Hesiod, both the gods and mortal men sprang from a single source. Once upon a time the deathless gods made out of gold a race of mortal men. They lived without sorrow, free from toil and grief; they did not grow old or weary and spent their time feasting; they had all good things in abundance, lived in ease and peace upon their lands rich in flocks; and when they died it was as though they were overcome with sleep.

But then there was a second generation which was made of silver and far less noble. For example a child would be brought up at his mother's side for a hundred years and remain a simpleton. But when they were fully grown they lived only a little time and that in sorrow because of their foolishness. They could not keep from sinning or from wronging one another, and they would not sacrifice to the gods. And so they were put away.

Then Zeus made a third generation, this time a bronze race of mortal men, sprung from ash-trees. They were in no way equal to the men of the silver age; nevertheless they were terrible and strong. They loved deeds of violence, ate no bread, and were fearful men and hard of heart. Great was their strength, and unconquerable. Their armor and their houses were made of bronze. They were destroyed by their own hands.

The fourth generation made by Zeus was "a god-like race of hero-men," men like demi-gods, the race before our own. These were the heroes who battled for Troy in Homer's *Iliad*. And others of them live still at the ends of the earth in the islands of the blessed along the shores of deep swirling ocean, "happy heroes for whom the grain-giving earth bears honey-sweet fruit" three times a year, "far from the deathless gods." And they have honor and glory.

Finally, Zeus made a fifth generation of men, "a race of iron who never rest from labor and sorrow by day and from perishing by night." Here Hesiod reports many of the ills of mankind: none will repay his parent's care, one man will burn another's city, none will keep his oath or refrain from violent dealing. The wicked will hurt the worthy man, and all will be wretched. Might will be right and reverence will cease. Bitter sorrow will be all that is left, and there will be no help against evil. Hesiod began the description of this fifth race of men (which he puts ironically in the future) by exclaiming, "Would I were not among them but either had died before or been born afterwards."

Authorities seem agreed that before Hesiod there was an earlier Greek myth of the four ages which he was reciting, that it may have come from the world-year of the Persian prophet, Zoroaster, which was divided into four quarters like the seasons. And that either he or someone before him had inserted the age of heroes between the third and last ages. For each of the four others are named after metals, while the age of heroes is not.

Two observations about Hesiod's account of the previous ages and his own are worth making. In the first place, he recognized that the central fact in previous ages were the metals even though the metals characterized the men rather than their tools, and even though he substituted gold and silver for stone and bronze. Was this in some way an idealized version of a folk memory? In the second place he recognized in his own age the importance of the use of iron.

Although Hesiod's account of the succession of civilizations is not cyclical and he does not anticipate a repetition of the cycle of ages, the impression remains that there could be a return to the golden age when men lived with pleasure and without pain. Hesiod may have owed something to a much more ancient Egyptian tradition of a golden age, which, however, did not return for the Egyptians either.

The Meaning of the Separate Ages

Men live poorly when they live without hope of some sort, if not for themselves then at least for their descendents. In every folk tradition there is the alleged "memory" of a golden age in the remote past, and many look forward to a golden age at some time in the remote future. This may be the source of the idea of a cycle of history, a return to the golden age. The Garden of Eden, known to us all, was such an age when no one was compelled to work and life was sheer joy. For the Greeks, in the period before Pandora opened her box, life was a kind of paradise as well. Both were in a sense golden ages.

In all likelihood there never has been a golden or a silver age. As we have noted, the work done in recent decades on pre-history show man to have been in his present condition for only 40,000 years. Before that we have clear evidence of more primitive types which were smaller, however, and no race of giants. There was a bronze age before the discovery of iron, and a stone age before that.

Life for early man must have been anything but easy. He was both hunter and cannibal, which means that he was a meat-eater but also eaten, and he lived precariously and probably for only a short time. It was not until the primitive societies of Daniel's and Hesiod's day that men dreamed of a better life in the past and—who knows—perhaps also in the future. What remains, then, is the notion of a cyclical history, of periods which repeat in time after the series has run its course. We shall find in later chapters that this is what happens to civilizations. The form recurs even if not the details, though these too are said to be similar.

The First Cyclical Account of History

The first truly cyclical account of history, in which there is a succession of ages which repeats by beginning again with the first age, is Plato's. He was no doubt influenced by the earlier account given by Hesiod.

Plato was born in Athens about 429 B.C. and educated there. At the age of twenty he became a disciple of Socrates and remained with him for nine years. The young Plato must have lived through the wars that Athens fought with Sparta, and, though we do not have any of the details, he may have fought in them. We can read out of the dialogues both a rich knowledge of the high theories of his time and a wide practical experience of the corruptions of political life.

When Socrates died, Plato is said to have traveled, with some intermissions, for twelve years—to where we do not know. We know that he visited Sicily and in Syracuse the court of the elder Dionysus, and he is supposed to have been sold into slavery on the island of Aegina, from where he was ransomed by Anniceris of Cyrene.

When he returned from Sicily in 386 he bought an estate near the precinct of the hero Academus and there founded a school, the Academy. The next forty years of teaching were interrupted by two visits to the court of Dionysus the Younger in Syracuse, where he tried unsuccessfully to help the tyrant establish an ideal state.

He died about 348 B.C. In his will, which has been preserved, he provided for his relatives and named his nephew Speusippus as the first head of the Academy which he had founded and which he must earlier have endowed.

In Plato's writings the ages of man are hooked up to the epochs of the astronomical universe. Changes in human life correspond to astronomical cycles, since all are parts of the one universe. Human cultures repeat a pattern of rise, climax, degeneration and end, with enough left at the end to begin the cycle all over again. There are several different accounts in his various dialogues. Though they are similar, they are by no means identical; I shall sketch them out separately.

The cosmic universe as a living thing was patterned on life,

Plato has told us in the *Timaeus*. Men, he said, notice night and day but not the movement of the planets which also takes place in time. The perfect world-year, which is 36,000 of our years, is completed when the planets all return to their starting point. In the *Statesman* Plato added that the world in alternate cycles revolves one way guided by God, then the reverse way from its own spontaneous motion. The source of all evil is the original chaos which existed before the cycles began. The order, which was introduced by the Creator, is the source of all good.

Plato admitted that he employed myth for the sake of the essential truths there were in it. In *The Statesman* he set forth his belief that the adventures of mankind follow closely upon the cycles of the universe. During a certain period God steers the universe and gives it order, but in another epoch when it has reached its allotted time he lets it go and of its own accord it turns backward in the opposite direction, and its disorder increases until he takes the helm again.

As it is with the universe so it is also with mankind. In the age of Cronus, the "hornless biped herd of tame walking animals" were earth-born rather than born from each other. There were then no states or families, for all men came to life out of the earth. They had fruit in plenty from the trees without the aid of agriculture, and they lived in the open air, for the climate was mild. Having nothing to do but eat and drink and converse with each other about philosophy, they were much happier than the people of later times.

So much for Plato's conception of early man. But, he went on, the people of that time soon were used up, the helmsman dropped the tiller, the earth turned backward, and another age was ushered in. It produced much disorder and evil, and little good, after the shock of the collision as the universe rushed off in the opposite direction. When the earth was turned once more into its present path of generation, in the age of Zeus, men were born from each other and families were created. When now a sufficient time had elapsed there was rest from disturbance and

confusion, and the world resumed its accustomed course in orderly fashion. Men tried hard to remember and practice the
teachings of the Creator, but succeeded only in combining them
with the previous harshness and injustice. At first they were
killed by wild beasts and could not take care of themselves, but
the Gods granted gifts: fire from Prometheus, the mechanical
arts from Hephaestus, seeds and plants from Demeter and
Dionysus, and these gifts marked the beginnings of human life.
Plato here clearly recognized the importance of material tools, of
artifacts.

In the *Republic* Plato mentioned the four ages of Hesiod, and
still thought they should be named after the metals, gold, silver,
brass and iron, but in Plato's version the four kinds of men were
contemporaries, a situation which gave rise to inequalities and
irregularities and so to hatred and war.

It came about in this way. The men of the iron and brass
ages wanted money and land and houses, but the men of gold
and silver preferred virtue and the ancient order of things. There
was tension and opposition between them until they reached a
compromise. The result was a government with peculiarities,
divided between the arts of peace and those of war.

In the *Laws* Plato hinted vaguely at an infinite past time and
at endless changes and transformations of life. The account here
is similar to the one in the *Statesman*, but more detailed.

There is truth, he wrote, in the ancient legends that tell of
floods and cataclysms and the periodic destruction of mankind in
their cities in the plain and along the sea-coast. After such a
flood there were left only hill shepherds, rustic survivors who
came down the mountain slopes. We must suppose that the arts
were unknown during ten thousand times ten thousand years,
and that no more than one or two thousand years have elapsed
since the discoveries of music and the lyre, not to mention numerous other inventions. Since all the tools and the knowledge
of their uses would have perished, the survivors would be unac-
quainted with the arts and the sophisticated life of the cities.

From these primitive survivors, wandering alone and afraid in the vast solitudes, have come all the civilization that we know. Progress was of course gradual, since everything had to be painfully relearned.

When men descended from the heights they cooperated out of loneliness and want. They possessed only a herd or two of oxen and a few goats. God gave them the art of molding and weaving, and so they had pots and clothing, but no iron or other metals, and so no way of felling timber. They had neither silver nor gold, yet they were not poor. They were good, and they lived by simple custom and patriarchal law.

In the next step they built a kind of population center by making loose walls at the foot of the mountains to guard them against wild beasts, thus creating a single large community. When many groups united in this way they chose a head to guide them by making a selection among the laws. By passing on what little they had learned to their children and through them to *their* children, they would find their way into a larger society with its own laws.

The Homeric poems, according to Plato, describe the third stage when Homer speaks of the founding of Ilium and other cities in the plain. Not knowing any better they put their cities where streams flowed from the heights, and under not very high hills for protection. In this third period they made war against Troy and in ten years overthrew that city. But the homes of the besiegers suffered; the youth revolted, and when the soldiers returned they were met with death, murder and exile.

And so we come to the prospect of a fourth stage which was once in process of settlement and continues so to this day. If only we could learn out of all this what changes make a state happy and what makes for the perfect city, we could begin again, Plato concluded.

In the dialogue *Critias* there is the memory of a war that had taken place 9,000 years earlier between the Athenians and their enemies from the kingdom which had been situated on the lost island of Atlantis. According to Solon, who had the tale from the Egyptians, Plato has told us in the *Timaeus*, the Athenians had an ideal state, and it was then that the inhabitants of Atlantis beyond the pillars of Hercules advanced to attack Europe and Asia and were only turned back by the Greeks, led by the Athenians, after the warriors from Atlantis had conquered as far as Libya and Egypt in Asia and Tuscany in Europe. Then, in one horrendous night, earthquakes and floods occurred in which Atlantis sank beneath the sea and most of the Athenians too were destroyed.

In these highly fragmentary accounts, retold on different occasions in a number of dialogues, there is a cyclical theory of history, one which embraces both the universe and in a corresponding way the races of mankind which periodically come up from primitive agriculture to build a civilization, only to have it destroyed again by wars, floods and other cataclysms. It is an incomplete account and hardly well organized, but it is there, and in our catalogue of attempts to understand the cycle of civilization it must be counted.

No doubt the Greek story of history, from Hesiod to Plato, owed much to the traditions handed down to them by the Egyptians. Plato said as much. The Greeks themselves were no more concerned with what had happened in the distant past than they were with what was to happen in the distant future. Of that vast Persian Empire, with which they had to deal on so many occasions and whose invaders they had to fight off at peril to their own survival, they had no knowledge and evidently wanted none. That certainly was another civilization but it did not interest the Greeks. So far as they cared, civilization as such was Greek and there could be no other.

Before the study of civilizations can be undertaken, it must first be recognized that the species exists, that, in other words, any civilization is only one of a kind. This thought never occurred to any Greek in classical times. They understood civilization only in terms of themselves, and considered all other peoples, the Persians included, as barbarians. The *idea* of comparative civilizations had to wait for many centuries. It requires a recognition of a civilization as one among many that the ancient Greeks did not have.

The writings of Daniel and Hesiod both came from primitive cultures. By the time of Plato we are in the midst of Greek Civilization. In this book we will be looking only at accounts of civilizations. But what distinguishes them from primitive cultures? Chiefly two developments: large populations concentrated in capital cities, and the production of manufactured articles. The Jews of Old Testament times and the early Greeks of Hesiod's day did not have much of either. The later Greeks did not have a large population but their productivity was immense. It is necessary only to recall the wealth of their architecture, their literature and their philosophy, to see the distinction. They had coins and some manufacture, vases for instance, and they traded with everyone in the Mediterranean. They were, in a word, civilized. But they still did not have the *idea* of comparative civilizations.

Chapter 4

St. Augustine's Religious Drama

Christian Civilization was the work of many men; it began with those who wrote the Old Testament and with the people they wrote it about, but it was centered on the New Testament. Jesus in the eyes of Christian doctrine was a man but he was also a God. It is well known that the Christian religion was an offshoot of the Jewish religion. From those two books came the set of beliefs to which all Christians are expected to subscribe. The Christian Church, though based on these beliefs, was something else. It was given a particular turn by St. Paul, who is generally credited with the institution. Our concern, however, will be with Christian Civilization, and we must look to its foundation in the work of St. Augustine, and in particular in one of his books, *The City of God.*

Augustine was born in North Africa in A.D. 354 of a pagan father and a Christian mother. He was brought up as a Christian although his baptism was delayed for some time. He learned Latin though not much Greek. In 370 his father was converted but died in the same year and the family moved to Carthage, where he studied rhetoric but by his own confession led a dissolute life; he acquired a mistress with whom he lived for over ten years and by whom he had a son. Also he became a Manichaean. The Manichaeans combined Persian and Christian elements of thought, and believed in two Gods: Ormuzd, the God of light and goodness, and Ahriman, the God of darkness and evil. Man's soul belongs to the good while his body belongs to evil; and so the struggle between the two Gods takes place also in man. It is an eternal struggle in which man is engaged. The elect of the religion were obliged to refrain from sex and meat-eating, though their followers were excused.

In 383 Augustine left Carthage for Rome, and subsequently taught both at Rome and Milan. After an intense moral struggle he was converted to Christianity in 386, and in 387 was baptized by St. Ambrose and returned to Africa. Back at Tagaste he founded a small monastic community, was ordained a priest by the Bishop of Hippo in 391, and himself made auxiliary Bishop of Hippo in 395.

The Roman Empire came to an end in 410, when the Goths broke through the frontiers and sacked Rome—an event that had a profound effect on Augustine, and may have suggested to him that there was an invisible City of God which belonged in heaven and could not be destroyed. He began his theory of history, the *City of God*, in 413 and completed it in 426. The barbaric disruption of the remains of the Roman Empire was continued for some time by the German tribes. Augustine himself died in 430 during a siege of Hippo by the Vandals.

The Two Cities

Augustine's theory of history involves the struggle between moral and immoral forces but is intensely individual. Man for him is nothing but will. Because of original sin the temptation of the devil, who had fallen before him, caused him to fall. Although evil is the absence of the good and not its opposite, the two behave like positive forces, and history is the stage on which the human drama is played out. It was in history that man fell from grace and it was in history that he was redeemed. Augustine's figure of speech is the image of the two cities, the City of God and the City of the Devil; his examples of these were the city of Jerusalem and the city of Babylon.

The spiritual world is split into two chief divisions, the realm of God and the realm of the devil. In the former are included the angels that have not fallen and the humans God has chosen for His grace. In the latter are all those not destined for redemption but left by God in a state of sin and guilt. There is a kingdom of heaven and a kingdom of this world. The two occupy in history a relation not unlike that of two different races which meet only in external action, while internally they remain quite separate. The community of the elect does not have a settled home on earth but lives instead in the higher unity of divine grace.

The community of the condemned, on the other hand, is ripped apart by discord; it engages in wars in its earthly kingdoms for the illusory values of power and rule. Augustine could see in the historical states of his time only the provinces of a community of sinners hostile to God and condemned by their miserable condition to quarrel among themselves. For him the kingdom of God was not of this world, but the Church remained the saving institution of the divine kingdom as the living presence of that kingdom in the midst of the temporal life.

In the *City of God* Augustine tried to combine an account of the Old Testament with that of the New Testament into a whole point of view, and thereby set Christianity on its way toward being a civilization. The emphasis, however, was on the life that was promised after death, and this world was to be endured only as a testing-ground for the fate of the soul. It was to be decided here and now whether after this life an individual was destined to go to join the angels in Paradise or to join the devil in hell.

God created the angels with free-will, by which they were able *not* to sin. The angel Lucifer, however, manifested the basic sin of pride, which means putting the love of self above the love of God. Lucifer gathered a following of angels who were attracted to his bad example. God then cast Lucifer (now called Satan) and his followers into hell. That is how Augustine says he interpreted the creation account of *Genesis* in which God separated light from darkness. Light is the name for the good angels who remained with God in his heaven, while darkness describes the fate of the bad angels who were cast down for their wickedness.

Why did God permit so much misery to happen to mankind? Surely, as we have seen, He had foreknowledge of man's sin and so could have prevented it. If He chose not to do so it was because He wanted to see what evil would result from the sin of pride and what good would come from His grace. The devil as a fallen angel hated and envied unfallen man, and so gladly engaged in tempting him to his ruin. God allowed this because he foresaw that in the generations to come, aided by divine grace, the devil himself would finally be conquered, to the greater glory of the saints.

For Augustine the world—by which he meant little more than the earth—is finite in time. It begins with God's creation as recited in *Genesis*, and it ends with the second coming of Christ and the Last Judgment. Before and after these events there was literally nothing. Men are deceived by lying documents which profess to give history many thousands of years, "when we find that not 6000 years have yet passed," Augustine insisted. He accepted that God had created the world in six days, as the authors of *Genesis* declared, and man himself on the sixth day.

In the beginning man was sinless and lived in an earthly Paradise in the Garden of Eden, but fell from his high estate through the misuse of his free will. If man had employed his free-will to choose the love of God he would have been rewarded with "angelic immortality" but instead he chose the love of self and was punished for his disobedience with death. He had been tempted to the sin of pride by the devil, who was jealous of unfallen man and so got the serpent to tempt Eve because as a woman she was the weaker of the two.

All men came from one man, Adam, and each inherits the sin of that man; in each of us there is a share of original sin. (Someone has pointed out that if you believe all men are descended from Adam then we are all equally Jewish.) Wickedness, Augustine declared, belongs to the will. In this way sin and evil entered the world. Man's fall from grace meant his expulsion from Eden. In this new condition he was infected with original sin and subject to total damnation. However, God in his mercy planned to redeem those who would accept salvation, and selected the Hebrews as the forerunners and the instruments of redemption. Mankind, however, went the other way, and became so corrupt and lost that God was compelled to destroy it by a flood, singling out for survival only Noah and his family. Later, despite this act of grace, the descendants of Noah returned to the ancient wickedness, except for a small number of righteous men who lived virtuously and in accordance with God's will. They were surrounded henceforth by a great mass of sinful and unrepentent humanity.

All subsequent human history is for the purpose of engaging in a struggle with the devil and his followers, the fallen angels and men who are unredeemed by God's grace. Among the inhabitants of the City of God were the great prophets and reformers of the Old Testament who continually rebuked the prevailing corruption of the world and bore witness to the approach of the Incarnation and the Redemption, an opportunity for all those living in the City of the Devil to turn away from their wickedness and so to be saved.

After the coming of Christ, those who gladly accepted him and his teaching and who lived according to his precepts were to be considered to be among the redeemed and counted as citizens of the City of God. Human history thenceforth was in essence the record of the endless struggle between the two cities, between the kingdom of God and the kingdoms of this world with all their pomps and circumstances, their vanities and seductions and their lusts of the flesh, and all that prevents mankind from embracing and following the new revelation. The outward and visible expressions of the two cities are, first, the Church which is the true home of the faithful and the dispenser of divine grace, and then, opposed to her, all those secular and material interests of mankind whose activities lead away from the spiritual and Christian life.

The suggestion that there is a City of God came to Augustine from the *Psalms*, especially 46 and 48, which of course he read literally. There is no origin credited for the City of the Devil except the evil that men do through the use of free-will. The City of God was formed, Augustine has told us, through the love of God, while the City of the Devil was formed through the love of self.

The warfare between the two cities, the City of God and the City of the Devil, will continue to be the meaning as well as the substance of human history until the second coming of Christ and the Last Judgment ends it all. After that there will be no more history. But meanwhile those righteous ones who have accepted Christ and repented of their sins will walk with God, receive their just reward, and live on in everlasting glory in the celestial City of God; while those who have rejected Him and led worldly, sinful and unrepentant lives will be eternally damned and cast once and for all in hell where they will suffer perpetual punishment.

In Book XXII, chapter 30, Augustine divided world history into eight distinct epochs: (1) from Adam to Noah and the Flood; (2) from Noah to Abraham; (3) from Abraham to David; (4) from David to the Exile; (5) from the Exile to the birth of Christ; (6) the Age of the Church, which corresponds with the Millenium of the Book of Revelation, and should be,

Augustine estimates, no longer than a thousand years; (7) the Sabbath, when the redeemed, the Saints, will rest in him; finally (8) the day of the resurrection of Christ, and the eternal repose not only of the soul but also of the body. There we shall rest and see love, and it shall be "in the end without end." The world, in short, is only the scene of man's alienation from God and of the struggles of man to return to God. That is its only meaning.

History or Myth?

Augustine's account, in which certain stories in the Old and New Testaments are treated as a reading of human history, certainly did furnish the background and the practical side of the doctrine of a Christian Civilization which prevailed in Europe for more than a thousand years, in fact until science as an institution arose to disrupt it. For the system to function so well, certain difficulties had to be overlooked. Chief among these was the question of foreordination. Elsewhere Augustine had asserted that God in his omniscience foresaw before the creation of the world that Adam would sin and what the consequences would be. God was able to do this because before the creation His mind knew the entire world of Platonic forms; He knew therefore all the events that would occur in His created world, all those that were as well as all that would be, and He created it nevertheless because He saw that it was good.

God by his special Providence controls all history. In this way He had selected certain souls to be saved and others to be damned from all eternity. But in that case what would happen to man's free will, and how would it be left to the human individual whether he wanted to be a citizen of the City of God and reap its heavenly reward after death or remain in the City of the Devil and suffer its horrible consequences in hell? This question was never settled, but somehow free-will was retained anyhow, and the individual's responsibility for his own choice of good or evil was left to him. It was only after eleven hundred years that Luther was able to interpret some of the writings of Augustine so that they seemed to justify the doctrine of salvation by divine grace rather than by good work.

It has not been sufficiently noticed that Augustine's case rests on the necessity for a certain kind of morality which the authority of the Old and New Testament can be made to support. It is no problem for the New Testament but it is for the Old. Augustine was particularly opposed to sexual intercourse, for instance, and attacked it as a sin time and again. Chapter 18 of Book XIV is entitled, "Of the Shame which Attends All Sexual Intercourse." *All*! Augustine found it significant that even lawful sex between husband and wife takes place in the dark and without witnesses. "This right action seeks the light, in so far as it seeks to be known, but yet dreads being seen." The carnal life involving any bodily indulgence is strongly condemned. It is permitted only to married couples and even then, one concludes, only when they desire to have children.

There is nothing in the Old Testament to support such a view. It is true that the Third Commandment condemns adultery, but the celebration of love and sex in the Song of Solomon certainly points to a joy and a celebration which is at odds with Augustine's view. The moralities of the Old and New Testaments overlap only at certain points but can hardly be made to authorize a consistent practice.

Christianity never did settle the question of just what the existence of the devil finally means. There is a paradox involved here and it has often been noted. Either God is all-powerful or he is all-good, for he cannot be both. Evil does exist in the world, no one questions that, and evil is inconsistent with God's goodness. Why then does God who is both all-powerful and all-good allow the existence of evil? The answer is that either God is not all-powerful, since if he were he would eliminate evil from the world, or he is not all-good, and therefore does not wish to do so.

Samuel Butler, the nineteenth-century English writer, once

observed that we have never heard the devil's side of the story because God has written all the books.

Christianity in the form given to it by Augustine was a myth. But it was a myth that brought about the Christian Civilization. We have to ask ourselves, therefore, just what the word, myth, means in such a connection. It means, I think, an emotional presentation of the truth. No religion was ever founded on falsehood; each one was believed by the faithful to be the absolute truth.

When I was a boy my mother was in the habit of buying me sets of books, a practice that was much in vogue at the time. One of these was called *Myths and Legends*, and the separate volumes dealt with different peoples, the *Myths and Legends of the Ancient Greeks*, or the *Myths and Legends of the Persians*, etc. It was not until many years later that I recognized with something of a start that what was discussed in these volumes were the *religions* of these peoples! "Myths and legends" were intended to mean "charming stories." No one pointed out to me that one man's myth is another man's religion. No doubt the Christian account of Augustine would have been read by another civilization, by the ancient Greeks or the Persians, for instance, as a charming story. A fanatic, I have come to see, is someone who believes very strongly in some other religion!

Christian Civilization

Christianity was the work of Jesus, but the Christian Church was invented by St. Paul and St. Augustine. One looks in vain either in the Old Testament or in the Gospels for the kind of puritanism that condemns all sensual and worldly pleasures. Jesus said he came into the world so that we might have life more abundantly, but Augustine viewed life on the whole as a wicked thing. Life in this world is only a trial and a preparation for life in the next world, a belief that was not calculated to make of life in this world a jolly affair. As one might have expected, under that dispensation life becomes rather grim, as indeed it must have been in the Middle Ages when ignorance, superstition, disease and dirt were the rule rather than the exception. There was no effort to achieve general education, since only the clerks and monks could read, as indeed had been the case in ancient Sumeria 4,000 years earlier. The Middle Ages in most respects represented a backward step to a more primitive stage.

What kind of church might have resulted from a stricter following of the saying of Jesus it is hard to guess. The overall effect of a reading of the Gospels is an overwhelming love of mankind. Jesus reminded us in Matthew 22 that to love your neighbor is no less important than to love God, a reaffirmation of Leviticus 19:18. But there are nevertheless some contradictions. Was the Jesus who preached love and passivity also the Jesus who drove the money-changers from the temple?

Certainly the wars of religion that Christianity has fought with its neighbors, the medieval treatment of the Jews, and perhaps worst of all, the internal conflicts, illustrated by the curse that the Roman Catholic Church and the Greek Orthodox Church officially pronounced upon one another, were hardly consistent with the teachings of Jesus. There has been little to equal the savage wars of extinction fought in sixteenth-century Europe between the Roman Catholic and Protestant wings of Christianity, which certainly were not what Jesus had in mind, even less than he had in mind the existence of a wealthy church within sight of many poor parishioners.

Augustine did not see the world in those terms. Like all convinced reformers, he was sure that the future would be better than the past. He persuaded Orosius, a young Spanish scholar, who had made a pilgrimage to him, to write a history, and it was to be a profane history, intended to show all the calamities which had been the lot of mankind before the birth of Christ. In his prologue, addressed to Augustine, Orosius says, "You ordered me to gather from histories and annals whatever mighty ills and miseries and terrors there have been from wars and pestilence, from famine, earthquake, and floods, from volcanic eruptions, from lightning or from hail, and also from monstrous crimes in the past centuries, and that I should set forth the matter briefly in a book."

A loaded argument, if there ever was one! With a selection like that, it was not going to be difficult to make out a case for a better future.

If we want to look at the Christian Civilization that St. Paul and St. Augustine actually built over the teachings of Jesus we shall have to examine the period which is known to scholars as the Dark Ages, that is to say, the period from the fall of Rome in A.D. 410 to the birth of Galileo in 1564, from the disintegration of the Roman Empire to the advent of modern Western Civilization as we have it now in Europe and America, a period of more than a thousand years.

There is, however, something to be said for the fact that Christendom was not consolidated as a civilization until 1100 when the wanderings of the German tribes were completed, the roving Normans were settled in England, and the first Crusade was undertaken. There was no unity in Europe before that date except what was furnished by the Latin language, the colloquial languages not having come into favor as literature. There was no organized society of any national dimensions, there was nothing in short that one could call a civilization.

The elements which went into the making of the Middle Ages were many and diverse. There was first of all the Latin inheritance; there was the still older inheritance of pagan elements from Greece; and finally there were the separate inheritances of the diverse groups which made up the population of Europe: the Italians, the inhabitants of Spain and Gaul, and the Teutonic tribes. Out of these elements running together there emerged a kind of common ground. Gregory the Great who died in 604 had reworked Augustine, and others had helped to prepare the way for a new synthesis. The names of Boethius and Isidore of Seville come to mind in this connection.

It was Italy, however, which led the way; after declining to a very low point it rose again with a new approach to its inheritance, for it was after all in Italy that the Roman Empire had seen its days of glory, and something of that influence still hung about.

Gregory was entirely occupied with religious matters but he interpreted them after the manner of the times. He believed in a profusion of miracles, and employed the method of allegory, whereby any event may be made to yield up a desired truth as a matter of necessity. He believed in the many appearances of the medieval devil in all of his deceitful disguises. He believed that through arduous prayer and worship the saints could be prevailed upon to intervene in worldly affairs to the devotee's benefit. Life, he thought, should consist in one long penance, and his description of hell was a kind of barbarized version of what Augustine had previsioned, brutalized and insisted on with great emphasis.

The romantic aspects of life in the Middle Ages have often been pointed out. There was some magnificent scholarship undertaken in the monasteries; there was the ordeal of the hermits; there was the devotion of the saints; there was feudalism and knighthood, and there was chivalry and courtly love. But there was a sordid side, too. What Henry Osborn Taylor has called, in a masterpiece of understatement, "the spotted actuality," left much to be desired.

There are many good accounts of life in the Middle Ages in Europe, and I will leave to others the description of the nobleman in his castle, of the knight and the merchant, who were not very much better off so far as animal comforts were concerned than the monk in his cloister or the ascetic in his hermitage. The secularized clergy with their vast material possessions and their active participation in the political life of the times were often the objects of cries for reform, and from the number of those cries we can guess something of the corruption which prevailed on all sides.

The feudal system was actually the product of a breakdown in general law and order, where every man individually powerless needed the protection of a lord. In return for the promise of military service the vassal secured his own refuge from attack by others, for despite the avowed following of the Man of Peace it was a time of violence. Peace is never a product of protestation but only of a social order which is preserved with common consent by an armed authority, and this can be as much "the King's Peace" as it can be the peace of a democratic government.

The feudal world was held together only by a general Christianity, not by a widely-established government, but in effect this did not work, not in any way that counted for the ordinary man. From the serf to the knight was a logical arrangement, but it had little to do with the Christian principles to which everyone gave lip service, even though it received the endorsement of baptism and the mass.

Christian Civilization did not do very much for the lot of its people at the height of its power. We must credit it, however, with tremendous achievements in the arts—the Gothic cathedrals, the masses of Bach and Mozart, the paintings and sculpture of the Renaissance, among many others; in literature not only the New Testament, but also Augustine's *City of God*, Bunyan's *Pilgrim's Progress*, Milton's *Paradise Lost*, Dante's *Divine Comedy*, and much else. It is difficult to wander among the monuments and museums of any country in Europe and not see the great power of Christian Civilization as it was for a thousand years before the coming of science. Science later created Western Civilization, which has its own wonders, but that is another story.

Many of the principles of Christianity were derived from the Old Testament and hence from the Jewish people. The book is not forgotten, but that there was a people behind the book sometimes is. In any case, one principle stands out above all others, and we must credit the Judeo-Christian tradition with having discovered and preserved it even if the practice has not properly supported it—the principle that asserts the infinite worth of every human individual. "Every human soul" is what the principle states, but then, in this world at least, the soul inhabits the body, and it is not possible to harm the one without hurting the other. This principle alone could save us all if we would only act accordingly, and move to preserve human life and to respect it whenever and wherever it happens. Perhaps even now it is not too late.

Chapter 5
Ibn Khaldûn's Universal History

Ibn Khaldûn, the fourteenth-century Arab, was the first man so far as we know to have the *idea* of comparative civilizations. His thoughts on the topic were very advanced for his time, and anticipate much later work. We know of no predecessors from whom he might have learned something of the thoughts for which he must therefore be credited, and if this is true it makes him all the more remarkable.

Ibn Khaldûn was born in Tunis in 1332. His family were descendants of a Yemenite tribe from the southern coast of Arabia, and had already lived for some time in Seville when in the tenth century the Muslims conquered Spain. Members of the family were active in the administration of Seville, but when that city was threatened by the Christians the family moved to North Africa, in Tunis they were welcomed at court and granted extensive land holdings.

We know little of Ibn Khaldûn's education except that he was exposed to the best that Islam then had to offer. For instance we know that he learned philosophy from the most important teacher in all of North Africa. He studied Muslim theology and law but also in the secular fields of logic, metaphysics, mathematics and astronomy. History was not the least of his studies, for his family was prominent in government, and history was important for those planning a political career.

Ibn Khaldûn's mature years were spent in the midst of the turmoil that existed in Muslim North Africa and Spain, and he moved from time to time between the North African cities of Fez and Tunis and the Spanish cities of Seville and Granada. At one point he was imprisoned for almost two years but managed to escape when a ruler to whom he was bound went down under an assassin's dagger.

Rulers often found favor in his learning and expertise, especially in the fields of law and government, but then they would be deposed and he would have to start over. On several occasions he fled back to Spain, but the failing struggle of the Muslims against the advancing Christians presented him once again with a prospect of combat; he was much more interested in ideas than he was in wars.

His practical experiences were varied. He held many administrative and judicial posts at one time or another. On one occasion he was in charge of a high court of justice and on another occasion he even rose to be prime minister. Frequently an adviser to governments, he had the opportunity to see the insides of many. One observer at the time described him as imposing, strong-willed and ambitious. When sent as an emissary to conclude a peace between the Christian king of Castile and Leon, and the ruler of Muslim Spain, he so impressed the former that he was offered the return of his ancestral holdings.

Later in Cairo he went with the ruler to repel a Mongol invasion led by the infamous Tamerlane. He was lowered over the walls to visit Tamerlane in his tent, and spent the next thirty-five days there in conversation with him. Tamerlane's interest was of course in learning about the weaknesses of Egypt and Spain. Ibn Khaldûn responded by writing a little book descriptive of those countries and was then allowed to return to Egypt.

Ibn Khaldûn's political fortunes fitted him perfectly for the task of writing a "universal history" which he undertook. He had been in Christian Spain and in varied Muslim domains of southern Spain and North Africa, and was able to follow their fortunes at first hand. Finally, he fell back upon the most advanced of Muslim centers, that of Cairo in Egypt. He had crossed the boundaries of a sufficient number of civilizations to make the topic of comparative civilizations almost natural to him. Beginning in 1375, he spent four years with his family in a castle near Oran occupied in study and writing. Later in Egypt he devoted such of his efforts to this task as could be spared from the duties of Chief Justice. He died in 1406.

It is on the *Muqaddimah*, the *Introduction* to his Universal History, that his fame chiefly rests. Completed in 1377, it remained practically unknown in Europe and the United States until recent times. Islamic scholars in North Africa were responsible for the rediscovery of Ibn Khaldûn's work as early as the sixteenth century, and they made much of it in the following two centuries; but it was not until the nineteenth century that it became known to Europeans and Americans.

Ibn Khaldûn's Approach to Human Life

Ibn Khaldûn never let his readers forget that man is part of the universe in which he occupies an intermediate position. He accepted the Ptolemaic astronomy of his day according to which the earth was the stationary center of the universe and the sun and visible stars revolved around it. The physical world both allows and limits human activity. Human society is therefore closely dependent upon the natural environment within which it exists. Ibn Khaldûn held long before Darwin that man "lifts himself out of the world of the apes, which have intelligence and comprehension, but have not reached the stage of deliberation and actualized thought."

That was the development below man, but there was another

and equally important development above him. He is related to the world of intelligences. Ibn Khaldûn believed that the rational faculty, with supernatural help, could communicate with the invisible world of angels and other spirits. Man can foretell the future, and gain the knowledge of things not known directly through the senses. The appearance of the Prophet was intended for eminently practical purposes. He brought a message from God and initiated laws to preserve and protect human society.

Ibn Khaldûn is careful to warn us, however, that the religious call cannot be effective without the solidarity resulting from group-feeling. "God sent no prophet who did not enjoy the protection of his tribe." The appearance of a prophet and his law is of essential cultural significance because he imposes new values and creates new institutions. That the prophet he referred to was Mohammed and the laws those set forth in the *Koran* is of course obvious.

History, said Ibn Khaldûn, is in reality information about human society, which is the culture of the world in its diverse aspects. It is concerned primarily with the nature and the causes of actual existence. The science of culture, by contrast, deals with real and possible existence. Culture is however not an independent substance but the property of another substance, man. Hence the natural character of culture refers to what is natural in man and differentiates him from the rest of the world.

Ibn Khaldûn gave as nearly as he could a naturalistic account of civilizations. In a period of great religious observance (to which, incidentally, Ibn Khaldûn himself subscribed) he managed to see the state as a secular and necessary institution. He thought that civilization was made possible primarily by its political organization. Culture is a result of human faculties and desires, not the desires of men considered in and for themselves but the conventionalized forms of social institutions erected over such desires, the totality of traditions and arts.

Man is part of nature, and the environmental conditions suitable for his growth must be temperate. Climates too cold or too hot produce brutes, not men. Primitive cultures are what Ibn Khaldûn called "communities of necessity." Primitive cultures are economic and based on land-holding. They are created when one social group overcomes others. Primitive cultures are always incomplete.

For civilizations he held that a great religion and great cities are required. Civilizations grow and develop; they must decline, and they must have endings. The forces that produce them may be hastened or slowed by chance or by design, but cannot be stopped altogether.

Ibn Khaldûn divided his study of civilization into a number of main topics. These were: primitive culture, the state, the city, economic life, and finally the sciences. We will follow his order and discuss first his idea of primitive culture and how it led to civilization.

The Origins in Primitive Culture

The development from primitive culture to civilization comes about in three stages. These may be described more or less in his terms as (1) the community of necessity, (2) the division of labor, and (3) the community of luxury. Each of these has its own peculiar accompaniments.

1. The simplest human needs are those men share with other animals and even with plants: food and procreation. In order to satisfy these needs they come together and make the tools and perform the many tasks required to produce food. To protect themselves against the attacks of wild animals they organize a communal defense and employ the faculties of the practical reason that other animals do not have. This is the community of necessity. A primitive culture is in a sense an incomplete culture rather than a complete but early form.

2. Once the primitive culture is established, however, it generates those forces which lead to its destruction. It comes about

in this way. Individuals are not capable of feeding and clothing themselves and producing the goods to satisfy all of their other wants. In order just to feed themselves they have to co-operate, and in this way they discover that each of them can do one thing better than the others, so he does it not only for himself but also for everyone. The division of labor leads to the production of more goods than are necessary for mere survival.

3. The resultant opulence changes the community of necessity into a community of luxury. Starting with the simple motive of preserving human life, men end with the business of transgressing the property of others and of what Ibn Khaldûn called "over-reaching" the limits of their own property. The result is a conflict in which the weapons, which were designed to subdue wild animals, are turned against other men, and bloodshed and confusion follow. Order is restored only when the most powerful leader subdues the others. By forcing them to accept his direction he becomes their ruler and so introduces kingship and establishes the state.

The Five Stages in the Life of the State

In the foregoing description of primitive culture Ibn Khaldûn tried to account for the way in which it led to the establishment of a state. The primitive culture goes through three stages, and the state goes through five stages. The development of a civilization is a consequence of the rise of a powerful dynasty, a sequence of rulers from the same family. The state is limited to extent by the dynasty's influence, it flourishes when the dynasty is at the height of its power, and it disintegrates with the disintegration of the dynasty. But it is the civilization rather than the state which makes it possible that most occupied Ibn Khaldûn.

1. This establishment of the state marks the first stage. In time the state becomes a community of sentiment when rule gradually shifts to dependence on desires and traditions. The

ruler has become an effective and accepted leader of his people. He is wise and just in his policies of taxation, in his defense of property, and in his provisions for military protection. He does not make too great a claim for himself because he is dependent upon the same group feeling which was responsible for his position in the first place and which continues to exist as before.

2. In the second stage of the development the ruler gains complete control over his people, claims autocratic royal authority for himself, and excludes others from sharing it with him. The people as a result become lazy, humble and servile, and begin to lose the solidarity of group-feeling. The instruments for the preservation of the state are threefold: the army, the public treasury, and a group of learned men.

3. In the third stage the ruler begins to rule for his own selfish ends. The purposes of the state become the satisfaction of the desires of the ruler and of his immediate followers. It is a condition of luxury and of leisure for the very few. The ruler concentrates on increasing his income, on beautifying the cities and erecting monuments and palaces. He is generous toward his supporters and pays his troops regularly. There is general economic prosperity. Under the new ruling class the arts and the sciences flourish. Self-indulgence and the pleasures of this world have become the only goals.

4. The fourth period is one of consolidation. The ruler is content with what his predecessors have bequeathed to him and he does not try to add to it. All customs and traditions are followed carefully, and for guidance everyone looks to the past. There is widespread satiation and complacency, a sense that the life of luxury always has existed and therefore always will continue to exist. There is an illusion of permanence.

5. In the fifth stage the ruler through his rapacity, his waste and squandering, succeeds in breaking down all that his predecessors had built up. His support, which now comes only from the lowest class, alienates the nobles and the gifted. The people come to hate him, and his support is threatened by the soldiers

who are no longer adequately paid because he spends the money for their wages on his own pleasures. High taxes discourage economic activity, while widespread physical weakness and moral vice make their appearance. The birth rate drops and there is an end to long range plans. Diseases and great plagues come to the over-crowded cities. It is the final stage of senility.

Ibn Khaldûn seems to have had in mind in these five stages only a single cycle. He did not provide for new civilizations to emerge from the old, as we shall see most later thinkers did. Only primitive cultures can provide the seed-ground and only one in fact did. In this sense he was thinking exclusively of the Muslim Civilization. But at the same time he seems to have thought of that Civilization abstractly, as though it could exemplify the form which all civilizations must follow.

The City as a Factor in Civilization

The city comes into existence as the result of man's desire for luxury, refinement and leisure, once his more primitive needs are satisfied, or so Ibn Khaldûn supposed. It is not intended merely to meet the need for survival, but requires the services of a large organization of men who are either rewarded for their work or compelled to work, and who must be protected while they are working. Only the state can furnish these elements. The character of the city takes color from that of the state which established or conquered it.

The city at first is engaged in a feverish expansion, but as it develops and becomes more prosperous a new social structure emerges. The new structure is characterized by the decline of natural solidarity which suffers a loss in both power and importance. As the luxury of the life of its inhabitants increases, their physical and moral virtues decrease. They depend upon the walls of the city and upon paid mercenaries to defend them, and they are helpless if betrayed. Their bodies are weakened by the absence of physical exercise and they are subject to the strains of civilized life. Prostitution and sodomy spread and the family as a consequence declines.

In the last stage of the city the state that had formerly protected it has become weak and helpless. If not attacked from the outside by enemies to whom it would fall an easy prey, it will disintegrate more slowly. Depopulation accelerates and the economic life of the city slows. There is less building and manufacture, and the unattended public works are allowed to slip into ruin. Demagogues, whose power base depends upon the rabble, succeed to positions of authority, while various factions in the city struggle with each other. Artisans and farmers, threatened by revolutions, produce less clothing and food, and famine appears.

Economic Life

Ibn Khaldûn was perhaps the first great thinker who saw the importance of business in the study of civilization. For him economics is tied to politics in an interesting way. The life of the city, as we have just noted, encourages the development of the methods of production of specialized goods and services. From the modes of production of primitive culture, which are merely those of farming, animal husbandry and hunting, the more civilized ways of the city involve industry, trade, elaborate skills, and exchange, with its use of money. It is the elaborate needs of the city that first encourage highly specialized manufacture. The state responds by facilitating such developments through a stable order of some duration, organizing an efficient bureaucracy and instituting special laws to protect economic activity. It both creates the needs for luxurious goods and services, and makes their production possible.

All of this can be arranged of course only by a ruling class that is responsive and understands the needs of the situation.

The growth of civilized economic activity is necessary to the rise of a great state, Ibn Khaldûn thought, and such economic life can occur only under the conditions made possible by the building of a large city. Trained artisans are attracted to the city where their work will bring high prices. This increase in the city population leads to an increase in the demand for skilled services and articles of value, and the increase in wages and profits leads to a further demand. The skills of the artisans are increasingly perfected, and ways are found to improve production. Professional traders appear who offer to transport goods and also to store them; often before selling they wait for a change in the market which favors an increase in demand and hence a rise in prices.

Economic laws and psychological motivation go hand in hand. General ruin is now in sight. Ibn Khaldûn saw that the development of specialization leads to an upward trend in prices. Luxury goods bring higher prices than do mere necessities, and hence their prices tend to rise more steeply. Goods manufactured for their exchange-value rather than for their use become popular. Monopolies appear, and profit is soon the primary economic motive. Raw materials begin to cost more, and transportation becomes more expensive. At the same time taxes are raised so sharply that they discourage production. Economic prosperity and the power of the state had grown up together, now they decline together.

The expanding bureaucracy, which had been an efficient means for maintaining the economic life of the city, has now become the end for which it operates. In order to support an expensive bureaucracy taxes have to be raised to a point where they discourage economic production. New taxes are devised, and the state itself begins to engage in commerce.

The normal operation of a competitive economy falls victim to the coercive power of the state. Producers and merchants are compelled to sell below the market price because they cannot compete with the state, which can buy at whatever price it chooses. Many traders lose their capital in this way and so are compelled to give up all economic activity. In the end it is a vicious circle, for there is a decline in the total amount of taxes collected, which results in the state's failure to meet its debts or support its vast bureaucracy.

With the decline in commerce and the general impoverishment that results, civilization decays, and life reverts to primitivism. Unemployment is widespread, and the consequent poverty leads to conditions which encourage famine and plagues. The citizens, in the hope of surviving, are reduced to stealing, murder and fraud of all kinds. Now that the economic support has been removed, the state is destroyed, and men fight again, only this time for mere existence; not any longer with hope but only from the fear of hunger.

The Sciences

When Ibn Khaldûn talked about the sciences as the fifth division of culture—with primitive culture, the city, the state and economic life, as the first four—he did not mean what we mean by the term. "Science" in those days meant formal study such as philosophy or mathematics; it could not have meant the experimental sciences, which had not yet been discovered.

The development of economic prosperity, Ibn Khaldûn declared, had widened the vistas of human experience. Their increased complexity compelled men to look for connections between the various parts of the culture. Such knowledge was at first practical but became theoretical at a more advanced stage. Thus on the flourishing of the sciences depended the prosperity of the state.

One effect of this development on the cities was the establishment of schools. In order that the knowledge gained in the practice of medicine and the other practical arts could be passed on, there had to be a formalization of the knowledge through the discovery of causal connections. The learned never gained the degree of wealth or influence acquired by those who engaged in commerce or politics, and so they tended to remain among the low-income groups.

When the state declined and the city with it, in the ways we have noted, then the sciences declined also. Men seeking to save themselves in a period of lessening power have little need for the luxury of the fine arts and think they have no need at all for philosophy. The schools suffer from neglect and may even be closed. The false sciences, like alchemy, are revived. Mystics and others who claim hidden knowledge counsel the masses against their legitimate rulers, and, by adding to the confusion in this way, accelerate the decline. Thus the sciences, once part of the glory of the civilization, now become a disruptive force and hasten its fall.

The Science of Culture

So much for the conception of the sciences which Ibn Khaldûn thought rose and fell with the civilizations. There was one science, however, which he believed was new with him, and that was the science of culture.

He began by distinguishing it from history. History, as we have noted, is an account of human society, whereas the study of culture in his sense is a science; it aims at disclosing the principles which underlie social events, and has the special task of guiding communities in the direction of the best regime.

History deals with *actual* existence, the science of culture with *possible* existence. History comes first, of course, and then the science of culture, which corrects historical reports and looks for true knowledge of the nature and causes of events. It does not try to correct but only to explain, and for this it seeks out the most fundamental elements which constitute culture.

Having considered the pattern of history—that is to say, the ways in which civilizations arise from primitive cultures and then grow, flourish, decline and fall—Ibn Khaldûn next had to look at civilizations apart from history. He felt that he must examine their separate structures and endeavor to see whether they have anything in common. In accordance with the thinking of his time, he supposed that the answer to his question lay in looking for the formal and material causes of culture. He sought an overall formal cause and subordinate material causes.

The formal cause of a culture, he wrote, is the state. The state is the principle of organization governing the whole of culture and lending the same character to each of its parts. That is the natural structure of a culture, and it shows the importance of the state. The material cause of a culture was for Ibn Khaldûn its institutions: its economic, religious, and educational subgroups, together with the men and tools peculiar to each. It is the state which determines their rank-order and their proper function.

Ibn Khaldûn distinguished more than one form of state. The differences between states was determined by the differences in the ends they pursued, their final causes. He distinguished three. A state could pursue the good of the ruled both in this world and the next; it could pursue only the good of the ruled in this world; or it could pursue only the good of the ruler in this world. He called the first the regime of Law, or the religious regime. The second and third he called rational regimes. The first regime was ordered by God through the legislation laid down by his Prophet (Mohammed). The second and third were ordered by man's own practical reason.

Ibn Khaldûn was careful to distinguish between the rulers of the regime of Law and the rulers of the rational regimes, that is to say, between the Caliph and the king.

The Caliph is the successor of the Prophet and continues his divine authority. Presumably, although the Caliph has this authority he must have also the consensus of the community. A community which consents to be ruled by a Caliph is one which admires his way of life. Under Islamic Law the Caliph must possess four qualifications for office: he must have knowledge of the Law, he must be just, he must be courageous in applying the Law, and he must be free of all defects of mind and body.

Thus there is in Islam both a Caliph and a king, although the Caliph remains in supreme authority over both religion and state. If the regime turns from being a regime of Law and becomes a rational regime, the roles are of course reversed. The office of king is now supreme, while the office of the Caliphate is either made subordinate or disappears.

Despite his respect for the traditional religion of Islam, Ibn Khaldûn's interests were primarily of this world and hence rooted in politics. You cannot successfully gain your end in the next world, he thought, without the exercise of proper behavior in this one. Therefore he was more concerned with politics than with religion, and it was his interest in politics which governed his theory of culture.

In this spirit he strongly preferred the first of the rational regimes the regime which pursues the good of the ruled in this world, rather than the second, the good of the ruler. The proper end of the rational regime, then, is the common good, and the task of authority is to promote the common good. The vizier must see to the affairs of state with this end in view; he must not promote his own interests but instead must exercise piety, liberality, courage and generosity.

Ibn Khaldûn was not an idle speculator but a knowledgeable thinker. He was concerned to examine states known to exist in history and with such patterns as he could learn from analyzing them. Unfortunately, there have also been examples of the second kind of rational regime, in which the end has been the good of the ruler. This kind of regime tends to serve the lower desires of the ruler and his unchecked appetites. He seeks ever to increase his power and to suppress, enslave and generally exploit the ruled. This is the very model of an unjust regime, and it is condemned by the Islamic Law.

The key word in the understanding of Ibn Khaldûn's ideas

about civilization is "solidarity," understood as the way in which men are held together by a common bond based on love and the desire for cooperation, somewhat similar to what the French call *esprit de corps*. It is a habit derived from the socially instituted form of one simple desire: the individual's affection for his fellow-man, and especially for his blood-relations. In short, solidarity derives from the family, yet it by no means ends there. The development runs from family solidarity to tribal solidarity, then to the solidarity of a whole people and finally to religious solidarity and the solidarity of urban groups.

What strongly dominates a culture once human nature has brought it into existence is its solidarity. There is nothing in human life as important as the bond between people. This is the primary cause that dominates all changes and developments in a culture. It is consistent with the final cause, which Ibn Khaldûn understood to be the production of the good. The end of society is the existence of good men.

Virtues and Shortcomings of Ibn Khaldûn's Account

When attempting to evaluate Ibn Khaldûn's contribution to the understanding of civilizations it is necessary first of all to remember that he lived in an age that was very different from our own. This has the advantage of giving us the material we need for a comparison. We do not have any studies of civilizations as wholes from the Indian Civilization or from the Chinese; these would have been of immense value to us. The view from the Moslem Civilization, and moreover from its Arabian wing, therefore serves us very well. It enables us to notice by contrast how very different our own is, and so prevents us from considering ours as the only one there has ever been. Provincialism in history is a common ailment, and we are not the only ones to suffer from it, as we are not the only ones to seek a cure.

Ibn Khaldûn did his best to lift himself by his own bootstraps out of a narrow view of man and all his works. Such an effort, I am sure, did not come easy. It bears all the marks of intellectual struggle and effort; and in many places we can see its failure. He could not imagine, for instance, how a civilization could develop a state with its cities from any beginning other than from a people who had come in from the desert. For it was the desert Arabs who were given the goal and with it the energy to form a civilization through the new religious inspiration of a new insight, if you will, a new Word of God in a message sent through His Prophet. And it came in a form simple enough to be understood by a people who had little learning and indeed no books. In the desert for a long time, the phrase "it is written" meant "it is true," hardly a statement that would be accepted by anyone who had the experience with the mass media that we have.

Thus there is much that is narrow and limited in Ibn Khaldûn's considerations of civilization. He had little global knowledge to call on and he thought that he was living in one of the world's greatest civilizations. Even given his small glimpse of Christianity and of the variety of Arab nations, he could not lift himself very far, not high enough to get the global view that his "universal history" required. But he was intelligent and he used the little knowledge that he had to great advantage. The very fact that he conceived of a universal history is certainly most remarkable for his day and age and for the emotions that usually go into any strong religious adherence.

There is something surprisingly modern about Ibn Khaldûn's view of civilization; in many respects it could have been written yesterday. Despite the large part that he knew religion played in the Islamic state, he saw it chiefly in secular terms. Its chief feature is its organization, which he distinguished in two ways.

The first, and most important way, as we have noted, was what he called solidarity, the bonds between the members which made them want to be associated. Social solidarity determines the group, whatever its size, be it a small tribe or a large civilization.

The second way, which could characterize only a large civilization, is the interdependence of diverse institutions. The economic, the military, the religious, even the state, all stand on the same footing with respect to the fact that they are equally parts of the one whole.

As to the state itself, he saw that it follows a steady development from its origins through the stages of growth and prosperity, to its decline and fall.

One of the great virtues of Ibn Khaldûn's view of civilization is its calm rationality. He thought that history is an independent science, even a social science, long before anyone else did. He condemned astrology because it is a false science, and was equally severe toward alchemy which, he said, is a fraud and a deceit. He was a fundamentalist in religion, however, and advised strict adherence to the Koran. He cautioned against the study of philosophy, which could be very dangerous to any man who had not previously armed himself by religious studies.

Nevertheless, the most important conclusion to be drawn from Ibn Khaldûn's world history is that he was the first to discover the connection between philosophy and civilization. He saw that philosophy is not entirely withdrawn from all other human affairs but has a definite field of application of its own. That field is the largest unit of human organization: culture, the whole of it. Plato had seen the same connection between philosophy and the state but he did not emerge with the same conclusions; for where Plato had looked at the connection from the point of view of philosophy, Ibn Khaldûn looked at it from the point of view of practical politics.

Only on the theory that a philosophy underlies every culture can we account for the common ground that holds together the different institutions in a state. This connection was one of Ibn Khaldûn's discoveries. Many centuries were to pass, however, before it was to surface again and then in the work of a thinker who at the time of his discovery owed nothing to Ibn Khaldûn and indeed had not heard of him.

When we look back over Ibn Khaldûn's work we come to a curious conclusion: that his mind outran his knowledge. He was capable of greater generalizations than his fund of information would permit. It is one of the few cases where we can say that if he had been born into the twentieth century instead of the fourteenth he would have outstripped the thinkers of our day who have concerned themselves with the study of civilization.

I say this because of what he did accomplish with what he had to work with. We must remember that in the fourteenth century what we now know as the modern world had not yet quite got under way. Much of the earth had not been explored; not many remote countries had been visited by travelers; the opportunity for the comparison of cultures and culture-traits had not yet opened up the large vistas that we know so well today; and yet Ibn Khaldûn saw the social scene in terms as broad as those we now use.

The French mathematician, Poincaré, once observed that genius consists in the ability to make a very little experience go a very long way, and if that is true then surely Ibn Khaldûn was a genius. His outlook was the most modern of all those thinkers who lived in the fourteenth century, the result of an excellent intellect, a mind capable of both imagination and great organization, a combination not often seen.

Belief in God is one thing, belief in a special Divine Law is another. The animals do not seem to need divine guidance in order to live according to their natures, and man does not have such guidance. When he thinks that he does, which is only too often, it is to set him against others who think that in a different way they do. As a consequence, almost all states have fought holy wars, which seems to negate their most basic intentions: to promote peace and harmony.

Ibn Khaldûn painted an impartial picture of how civilizations rise and fall, based on the conditions within the state. Despite the conquests of Islam which had taken place before his day and were to continue after, he gave little thought to external relations. He gave full credit to all the elements that go to make up a civilization but admired chiefly the arts of peace. The odd thing is that he managed to see a state in which an established religion is the most potent force as one that could be moved chiefly in secular terms. The religion of Islam, if the Koran is any evidence, approves of the conquest and death of all those who resist conversion. This is not the Islam that Ibn Khaldûn had in mind when he considered it in terms of the ideal civilization. Yet he was one of the great contributors to what remains still in our own day a very young study.

Chapter 6

Vico's New Science

In 1935 Philip Mairet, the editor of the *New English Weekly*, asked me to review a book by H. P. Adams on *The Life and Writings of Giambattista Vico* which had just been published by Allen and Unwin. Stanley Unwin was my publisher then, too, and I was in London at the time, and so I undertook to do it. The result was that I became very interested in Vico. I don't have Italian (nor very much else, in fact; and when I am in England I sometimes suspect that my hold on English is not too strong, either); but anyway I found that there was an abridged French translation of the *Scienza nuova* (the *New Science*) by Michelet. I read it in French.

It had a far-reaching influence on my life. I wrote an appreciative essay on Vico—my way of finding out what I thought about him—and in this way I was introduced to the study of history. It was indeed astonishing that Vico's principal work had never been made available to an English audience. A few years later I tried to get Stanley Unwin to publish a translation of the *Scienza nuova* but he wrote me that, while he thought the project an admirable one, Mussolini had chosen just that week to threaten to sink the British navy and this seemed no time to try to interest the English public in an Italian philosopher. I thought the fact that Vico had flourished in the eighteenth century would take the heat of the current crisis off him, but I was wrong, or so Mr. Unwin informed me. But in any case the project of an English translation of the *Scienza nuova* was summarily dropped, and no English translation appeared until Bergin and Fisch did theirs in 1948; it was published by the Cornell University Press.

Giambattista Vico was born in Naples in 1668, the sixth child of his father's second marriage. His father was a happy though illiterate bookseller, his mother strangely melancholy. At the age of seven a fall from a ladder knocked him unconscious for five hours. Idiocy or early death was predicted for him by the attendant surgeon, and convalescence kept him from all formal education for the next three years.

He was educated, after the custom of his time in Italy, by Jesuits. His studies were chiefly in Greek philosophy and Roman law and history. From the Greek philosopher, Plato, he learned how things should be. Plato's dialogues are often devoted to descriptions of the ideal of conduct for individual man and societies. From the Roman historian, Tacitus, he learned how things really are. Scandals and frightful savageries abound in the pages of Tacitus.

In 1699 Vico was appointed to the Chair of Rhetoric at the University of Naples. Most of his life was spent in poverty, his academic posts not bringing in much in the way of financial remuneration. The *New Science* was first published in 1725, and appeared again in a much revised edition in 1730. He died in 1744. After many unsuccessful attempts to improve his academic status, he devoted most of his time to the successive editions of that work. He died in 1744 while preparing a third edition.

Vico's reputation rests on the second edition of the *Scienza nuova*, the *New Science*. It is divided into five parts, devoted respectively to philosophical first principles, the universal history of barbaric society, the discovery of the true Homer, the science of national history, and the medieval illustration of the law of reflux (or return).

The seventeenth century was a transitional period. The medieval world was coming to an end and the modern world was being born. Transition figures have a certain advantage, for they can look in both directions and find interesting suggestions of quite different and even contrasting sorts. Vico had a great respect for the old Roman Catholic religion—and also for the new experimental science. He tried to incorporate the best of both worlds in his work, and to some extent he succeeded.

What he set out to show in his *New Science* was that there is an ideal eternal history which every nation traverses alike through separate stages. This history is made by men, he said, and so what more fitting than that it should be described by a man, since its modifications took place within the human mind. The new science which he had created, Vico thought, proceeds exactly like geometry, only instead of lines, planes and figures, it deals with human affairs.

The Three Great Ages

Vico's theory of civilization is the first of the truly cyclical theories. History presents an ideal eternal pattern, "the ideal of the eternal laws in accordance with which the affairs of all nations proceed in their rise, progress, maturity, decline and fall, and would do so even if there were infinite worlds being born from time to time throughout eternity."

The cycle of civilizations started, Vico declared, with an Age of the Gods, which lasted nine hundred years. There were giants in the earth in those days, such as the Cyclops of Greek myth, and he thought there was evidence that human history started with such creatures. The story of man began after the flood described in the Bible, when the descendants of Noah roamed the earth, without their religion, lost from one another, pursuing shy and unwilling women, and fleeing from the wild animals that roamed the forests. These wild men scattered in search of food and water, and grew large because of their savage life, giants without a language except a few gestures.

· The transition from the brute level to the human, Vico went on, was effected when these creatures sought refuge from thunderstorms and found in caves shelter from the terror occasioned by the lightning. A permanent dwelling led to an ordered sex life. Instead of the community of women which had been the arrangement in the beast-like state, men now settled down with particular women, and "through fear of the apprehended divinity, in religious and chaste carnal unions they solemnized marriages under cover, and begat acknowledged children and so founded families."

They began to bury the dead and believed in the immortality of the soul. Religion, Vico thought, is fundamental to social organization and so furnishes one of the basic principles in the development of any civilization. It was at this stage also that men acquired self-consciousness and became responsible moral beings. Family life and religious awakening led to the development of a language. Reason was weak though, and imagination strong, he said, hence the importance of poetry.

In these ways the Age of the Gods was followed, in Vico's account, by the Age of Heroes, ushered in when the fathers of families subdued the giants, the beast-men who were still living in the savage state, and made slaves of them. Competition between the rulers of households began, and some of the subjugated peoples won democratic rights. The dependents were without gods and so could neither rule nor, since they could not marry, form families of their own. Government remained the business of the few civilized men who were members of the aristocratic class. Feudalism was the social order. Trade and commerce were introduced and, with them, war. In this Age people "looked upon each other as perpetual enemies, and pillage and piracy were continual because, as war was eternal between them, there was no need of declaration."

The third and last of the ages was the Age of Men, the period of the Greeks and Romans, an age of humanism; all men recognized themselves "as equal in human nature, and therefore established first the popular commonwealths and then the monarchies, both of which are forms of human government." Jurisprudence and law were for the first time based upon principles of equity and truth; secularism and naturalism were dominant. Reason and philosophy were cultivated, and so was knowledge of the laws of nature, of man and of human societies.

The Age of Men had two eras, first the era of the free popular commonwealth, such as the democracies of Greece and Rome; then the era of monarchies. The trouble with democracies is that citizens are too engrossed in their private concerns and in procuring luxury goods. Because of this egoism, public affairs become less and less a matter of interest. Vico spoke of a "natural royal law" and of the development of monarchy out of democracy on the basis of two principles: the providence of God and the utilities of social life.

In his view, therefore, monarchy marks a higher stage of human development than democracy. In ancient times, Vico wrote, Augustus saved Rome from the dissoluteness of the Republic. Monarchies are by nature popularly governed, both through the laws by means of which the monarch seeks to make all his subjects equal, and through the royal possessions by means of which the monarch humbles the nobles and keeps the masses free from their oppression. "Monarchy is the form of government best adapted to human nature." Vico was in no danger of being thought a revolutionary.

The second era of the Age of Men is the end of the cycle of history. After that there is a return of the conditions which prevailed in the world and which led to the beginning of the Age of the Gods. Vico called this a *recorso*, a reflux or return; his theory was truly a cyclical one.

At the end of the Age of Men, when they cannot agree upon

a monarch and live in a state of decadence worse than any monarch could remedy, a nation was either conquered by another and stronger nation or else it took refuge in what Vico described as an "extreme remedy." Men thought only of their own private interests, and, though living together, they had once again begun to behave "like wild beasts in a deep solitude of spirit." A period of civil wars turned their cities into forests and the forests into the dens and lairs of men.

Thus as a result of centuries of barbarism men had changed themselves back into uncivilized animals and reached a "point of premeditated malice," by which they were "stunned and brutalized, sensible no longer of comforts but only of the sheer necessities of life." This return to barbarism meant that "the nations had dissolved themselves, and their remnants fled to safety to the wilderness, whence, like the phoenix, they rise again." We are now then at the outer edge of the Age of the Gods, which is soon to begin anew.

The example which Vico gives of this endless cycle begins after the fall of Rome and at the end of its Age of Men when the barbaric invasions of the German tribes brought back an Age of the Gods. The feudalism of the Middle Ages in Europe was an Age of the Heroes. Dante was the Homer of the Heroic Age in Europe. After his *Divine Comedy* had closed that Age, the Age of Men began again with the European monarchies and democracies. Vico hinted strongly that after the European Age of Men had run its course, there would be another barbarism, which as usual would usher in another cycle of the three Ages.

Most of the time Vico kept close to his threefold divisions into the barbaric society of the Age of the Gods, the heroic society of the Age of the Heroes and the civilized society of the Age of Men. He devoted many pages of his work to showing by contrast how certain elements in society had shifted accordingly. For example, authority was vested first in the gods, then in the senate and finally in the monarch. Judgments were based first on divine law, then on the law of nations, and finally on the truths of fact. Government was at first theocratic (we would say based on an established religion), then dictated by an aristocracy, and finally headed by a king.

Some of the classifications are amusing. For instance, at first customs are religious and pious, then "choleric and punctilious" (that is to say, irritable and involving strict observance), and finally dutiful. Language was confined at first to divine ceremonies, then to "heroic blazonings" (symbolic pictures, as in the knights' coats of arms) and finally to articulate speech.

There are also passages where the development of civilizations is more finely divided. For instance there are examples of traits which are five and even six in number. Two examples of five: "The nature of peoples is first crude, then severe, then benign, then delicate, finally dissolute." And again "In the human race first appear the huge and grotesque, like the Cyclops; then the proud and magnanimous, like Achilles; then the valorous and just, like Aristides and Scipio Africanus; nearer to us, appear those imposing figures with great semblances of virtue accompanied by great vices, who among the vulgar win a name for true glory, like Alexander and Caesar; still later, the melancholy and reflective, like Tiberius; finally, the dissolute and shameless, madmen like Caligula, Nero and Domitian."

A last example of six: "Men first feel necessity, and then look for utility, next attend to comfort, still later amuse themselves with pleasure, then grow dissolute in luxury, and finally go mad and waste their substance."

The NEW SCIENCE *as a New Science*

When Vico looked backward toward the Roman Catholic tradition of Christianity, he felt just as pious as did Descartes, the effect of whose work was to scuttle it. Forward with Descartes lay the new development of the sciences, which caused men to look at the world about them and to value only the evidence of the senses, where religion had insisted that, when revelation contradicted reason, it was possible to believe what is absurd.

That Vico with all his piety thought he was constructing a new science of history—we should say, a new social science—is undeniable. Although, as we have seen, he asserted that "our science describes an ideal eternal history traversed in time by the history of every nation in its rise, progress, maturity, decline and fall" and that "it has and will have to be" like that, still it is true also that "this world of nations has been made by men, and its guise must therefore be found within the modifications of our own human mind." Furthermore, "our science proceeds exactly as does geometry." These ideas he somehow seems able to reconcile in his thoughts with the fact that it is "providence" (a name surely for God) which works through "the order of civil things," and with the belief that "if one is not pious he cannot really be wise."

In a final burst of piety Vico did in fact forsake the entire work which he had written, a work in which everything in an age was held to be relative to everything else. In the concluding pages of the *New Science* he insisted that "religions alone have the power to cause the peoples to do virtuous works by stimulation of the senses, which alone move men to perform them." Religions in the past and future may be relative to the civilizations of which they are parts; that is to say, all but one. "There is an essential difference between our Christian religion, which is true, and all the others, which are false." No cycle of civilizations there! However, that is not the whole story. Vico did look at history in a new light and had some unique and valuable things to say about it.

The obligation to demonstrate the historical development of his triadic cycles led Vico to examine the earliest primitive society. We know scarcely anything of this topic today, but what little we do know is founded upon archeological researches and excavations. Vico knew less and, moreover, leaned for his knowledge upon such doubtful sources as the deductions from his own hardly founded theory and from sacred texts. The result was the primitive man of H. G. Wells and the modern Sunday supplements, a primitive man as close to oysters and apes as to civilized man—in short, a convenient piece of fiction. The flood, the race of giants, the relapse into the stage of "nature," and all the rest of Vico's fanciful mythology must provoke a smile, but a smile at least of sympathy for the tremendous effort to interpret anything from the few facts which he had from the earliest of human ages.

Vico's struggles with prehistory were not altogether as fruitless as his conclusions would lead us to believe. He was not as tempted as previous historians to find only virtues in ancient history. The study of history had brought forth in Vico's work several clear methods for discovering historical truths. He found that language is a fruitful source of ancient customs and institutions. Many abstract words can be referred back to their origins in actual situations among earlier peoples. He also found that myths and legends are symbolical of beliefs. Finally, he understood that anything which remains buried under the social inheritance, however trivial—whether the wisdom of common speech, the warnings of superstition, or the recountings of folk poetry—may serve equally as hints of ideas once held and of conditions that had prevailed.

The heroic society according to Vico contained not the slightest trace of democracy, not the smallest amount of social feeling. The heroes were the sworn enemies of the common people, and their stern virtues, which resulted in cruelty, combat and self-discipline of the severest kind, contained nothing of human sympathy or warmth. Thus the heroic morality, although an advance over primitive society in that it *was* a morality, was based on force rather than justice, or rather on a justice consisting of force. In the heroic society, families were more important than states, states more important than any wider community; the period was one of extremely limited societies bound down by poetical language to the immediate neighborhood.

The greatest recorder of the heroic society continues to be Homer. Vico pointed out that the heroes of the Homeric legend behaved just like heroes; anti-social, rude, obedient to their moral code, thoroughly unsympathetic and wild. The partisan gods, too, were not unlike the heroes they occasionally defended. Brute force was the only argument they were capable of understanding. The vastness and inclusiveness of the Homeric poems led Vico to suspect that they were not written by any one person, but that the term "Homer" meant simply a collector of legendary ballads. Thus Homer came in Vico's mind to stand for the heroic Greek, and his poems to represent the customs and institutions of barbaric times.

The rise of democracy from this heroic form of society as described by Vico is very Marxian, for it consists in the opposition of economic classes. The common people, the plebes and slaves, who under the heroes have either been neglected or oppressed, begin to clamor for their rights as a majority. The heroic society contains in it the elements necessary to bring about its own overthrow. The conflict thus undertaken between the oppressors and the oppressed results finally in the formation of a popular democratic government.

The popular democracy, however, is partially self-defeating in its aims; for it is incapable of any good higher than that of equality and common interest. Thus it passes severe laws, and wages a series of destructive wars, until another change in government is rendered necessary. This later form is that of a perfect monarchy: a democracy conducted by a single ruler for the good of all. Vico here sounds as though he considered fascism an advance over democracy, but such is not the case. His monarchy is an impossible ideal, presupposing an enlightened leader and, as Croce points out, might even be said to be "a new form of popular government." The monarch is not to be the instrument of oppression but of opposition to it.

Whether or not we agree that Vico was elevating the monarchy to a necessary and preferable position, it is easy to see that he was led to do so by deriving from Roman history the principles of all history. The succession of primitive, heroic, democratic and monarchic societies, namely Polyphemus, Achilles, Aristides and Caesar, are taken from Roman history. Vico indicated a direction and suggested a method which may be more successfully employed when more facts are available with which to operate.

The Middle Ages were for Vico an excellent illustration of his cyclical theory of history, being a second barbarian or heroic age. The barons and knights represented the heroes with their few but rigidly adhered-to laws, while the serfs represented the slaves. Social feeling disappeared and "noble virtue" took its place. Language fell back into the symbolic stage, as witness the widespread use of coats of arms. The Middle Ages were so perfect an example of the "reflux" of heroic society that they even had their Homer in the person of Dante. Thus Vico was among the first to recognize in *The Divine Comedy* its great social significance.

It is difficult to learn Vico's opinion of his own times, but there are a few hints. He was indeed a reactionary, but a reactionary only insofar as the true revolutionary reformer finds elements from the past which can be fitted into an ideal future. Vico's criticism of his own age took the form of an attack upon the system of education of his day, and this fact too is revealing. A true transition figure, faced in both directions yet emerging with a synthesis rather than a discord, he felt keenly the failure of contemporary education to weld into a whole the medieval logic which had survived and the new mathematics which had not yet been put to work. Although his attitude was profoundly pessimistic, his writings may be said to have contained all the promise necessary for the future.

At times Vico presented the basis of social science as though it were wholly psychological. He maintained, for example, that the world of the Gentile nations was certainly made by men. At other times, the basis is presented as a wholly realistic affair, a search for ideal possibilities. Despite serious difficulties one is able to see in Vico's work as an entirety exactly what he was trying to do. He was attempting to establish social science on a medieval foundation. That is why he hesitated so often to make an absolute choice between science and Christianity, which he then thought, in common with everyone else, was represented by the choice between Descartes and Plato. Vico did conceive history, as Professor H. P. Adams pointed out, as "the temporal expression of ideas that are eternal." Vico himself says that these ideas are an "ideal, eternal history which has its course in time."

What Can We Learn from Vico?

The value of Vico's work for our own period remains to be seriously explored. The principal problems with which Vico was confronted still bar the path of progress; but today, because of large population increases, they have grown more insistent. The petty royal rivalries of Vico's age have been replaced by larger and more dangerous economic upheavals. Further, the brilliant success of the physical sciences has made it obvious, more than social failure alone ever could, that the immediate task before us is the establishment of a valid social science.

In the various unconnected hints of the *New Science* we may find a way out. Vico believed in the possibility of social science and thought that he saw in the vitality of current events, with all their evil, failure and misery, a justification for God. He was, in short, groping always toward a theory which he himself was never able to formulate, *viz*, that the subject-matter of social science consists in independent values.

I don't know what makes a productive thinker, and I don't think anyone else does yet. I would like to show, if I could, all the equipment which a productive thinker must have, but I offer only a sample. Culturally speaking, one type of productive thinker is the man who emerges successfully from the struggle between two traditions because he has been able to extract his own contribution from them. Vico's work shows the strong innovations of the Renaissance, as for instance when he talks about the "creative" aspects of the human mind; but as we have seen he was also a good Roman Catholic, and so he liked to see this capacity as God-like. Both God and man, he said, manufacture the truths that they know, and by knowing make them true.

The result was a curious mixture of influences. Consider how Vico treated certain of the large cultural undertakings: philosophy and religion, for example. Philosophy for him gets itself established through religion, and religion is central in society. The primary law is the existence of providence, but providence works through what Vico called "the economy of civil things." It is providence, then, which ingeniously enough, is responsible for the way in which chance serves necessity.

Many productive thinkers discover a field of inquiry in the very act of making a contribution to it; and it often happens that the discovery of the field exceeds in importance the value of the contribution. This is what I think happened in Vico's case. Vico had forerunners, chiefly Hesiod, Plato, St. Augustine and Ibn Khaldûn. But Hesiod's theory was mythological, Augustine's was a religious view of the philosophy of history and Ibn Khaldûn's was not well known in western Europe until recently.

Vico, therefore, deserves the credit for having introduced the philosophy of history into western culture. He drew heavily for suggestiveness on the Hesiod of the *Works and Days* and on the Plato of the *Statesman*. Plato's account is one of cycles with the details left vague, and still sounds remarkably modern, but it is primarily Vico who deserves the credit for having established the study of history as a special field of investigation.

Vico's principal contribution to the sum of valuable ideas lay in his belief that a universal history is possible. There is a lifecycle of civilizations just as there is of all living organisms, and it can be studied in the details of its structure. If successful in its study, we would then have an instrument which would enable us to predict to some extent the future of our own society.

No doubt we will have difficulty in giving credit to a thinker whose ideas now seem commonplace; but that is precisely because those ideas have been so thoroughly accepted. Vico saw that civilizations differ with respect to the degree of advance, but he understood the progress in only three stages.

We have come to recognize in his "Age of the Gods" the primitive family of the nomadic hunting culture which was prevalent in what we have now discovered to be the hundreds of thousands of years before settled civilization. His "Age of the Heroes," taken chiefly from Homer, was that of the first settled communities, and was a description chiefly, he thought, of the struggle for power between the conservative class of rulers and the revolutionary class of citizens pressing for equal rights and a greater share of goods. Finally, his "Age of Men" is that of a civilization roughly like ours, modelled on the Roman Empire, in which there was a civil society ruled by respect for law. The fourth stage is a return of the first, and occurs when the third stage breaks down.

This is crude enough but there was more that was suggestive. For his primitive society, his heroic society and his civilized society all had in common a set of traits. All had some kind of human nature, some set kind of customs, some kind of law.

Vico's conception of the three temporal epochs of gods, heroes and men is of course no longer acceptable. But as he saw it, the movement from the divine through the historic to the civil is more than a mere succession of cultural states. It marks arrival at the stage where man is placed in his own care. Once upon a time the gods had been the only restraining influence on the ferocious nature of man, then there were later substituted the political conditions based on brute force, and finally we come to the principles of justice as embodied in man-made law.

A certain measure of disbelief is necessary to the continuance of inquiry; tolerance is the result of noting that there are ways of doing things other than our own. This approach is emphasized by the possibility that there could be a more perfect civilization than any which has existed. It certainly does point the direction in which we should press our efforts. Vico may have known only two civilizations, the Hellenic and the Italian, but look at what he was able to see by comparing them, using Greek achievements as a key and the history of Italy as a model!

That there was an element of the ideal in such a manner of formulation he would not have denied. Indeed he saw clearly that the ideal and the actual are different but related. They are in fact two worlds, and each requires the other for its explication, the world of what-ought-to-be and the world of what-is. Plato, in Vico's system, stood for what-ought-to-be and Tacitus for what-is. It is one of Vico's great and neglected insights that the idealist and the materialist can make common cause. He was also the first to insist on the idea of civilization as a single organization, with its social institutions governed by its range of possibilities, but with some degree of freedom still left to the individual.

The advance of civilization is across such a broad front that it is often difficult to trace the effect on it of a single force, such as the ideas put forward by Vico. He influenced the historians more than he did the social scientists. He taught them both that history can be looked at in the round as a coherent whole.

But if you say "Vico" today to anyone interested in literature, he immediately thinks of James Joyce. Joyce made his living for years as a language teacher in Trieste, and it was perhaps there that he made the acquaintance of the work of Vico which had become much known at that time outside of Italy. The monumental achievement of Joyce in his two great books, *Ulysses* and *Finnegans Wake*, owes much to Vico's idea of the eternal return.

Chapter 7

Hegel's Ideal Germany

One of the most profound (often one of the most irritating) thinkers in Europe was the philosopher, George Wilhelm Friedrich Hegel. You can tell how important he was from the puzzling fact that within the last century his work has influenced both the communists and their arch enemies, the idealists, two groups who thoroughly loathe each other. Materialists, like Karl Marx, have said that they owed a great debt to Hegel, and so have the idealists, like the English philosophers, Bradley and Bosanquet, who thought that reality is mental. Revolutionists and conservatives alike have said that they found arguments in Hegel's writings which they thought justified them.

The lives of most philosophers are uneventful, and Hegel's was no exception. Born in Stuttgart in 1770, he was an ordinary student at school and entered the University of Tübingen at the age of 18 to begin the study of theology. While there he engaged in lively discussions with some of the students on the issues involved in the French Revolution.

After he left the University he became a private tutor for six years, first in Berne, then in Frankfurt, and in 1801 he was appointed to the faculty of the University of Jena. He finished his first great book at midnight before the battle of Jena in 1807, which closed his University. He married in 1811 and supported his wife and himself by becoming rector of a secondary school at Nurnberg, where he remained until 1816, when he joined the faculty of the University of Heidelberg. Two years later he was honored with the chair of philosophy at the University of Berlin, where he taught until he died of cholera in 1831. He was only 61.

The Nature of History

Hegel was a philosopher whose theory was surprisingly simple for all of the complications he made of it. He believed that thought and events move in the same way, though he took his model from the movement of thought. Any thought could give rise to its opposite, and then the two of them in turn gave rise to a third which incorporated the best of both. He called this movement in three parts a "dialectical" movement, and he saw it at work everywhere, equally in nature and in social conflicts.

Wherever Hegel looked he saw nothing but three of a kind. He saw geography that way, for instance. There were always arid lands, valley plains and coastal regions. Africa was divided into the area below the desert, the area above the desert, and the Nile River delta. Usually, however, the third was the synthesis of the earlier two. His division of European history into ancient, medieval and modern periods, was adopted and is still in general use today, though it has serious limitations.

Reason governs the world, Hegel announced, and so it is not too surprising to hear him say further that world-history is a rational process. He did not mean by reason human reasoning, he meant something like it, but more a reason that is imbedded in the world, as though thought were external to man and a part of all events, the social included. The laws that govern the universe and the reason that governs man are one and the same kind of thing, and it is the same reason which operates also in the social sphere.

The key to the understanding of world history is, oddly enough for Hegel, the idea of freedom. History, he said, is moving toward a purposive end, and that end is freedom.

But I am afraid that when you come right down to it what Hegel meant by freedom is not what anybody else means. He meant the willing acceptance of constraints. Paradoxically, Hegel's freedom turns into its opposite: necessity or law. But if you had pointed that out to him, he would have agreed. Does not everything turn into its opposite, he would have asked? As we shall see, there is some logic as well as a little hint of madness in such a viewpoint.

History, we are told, is the account of the life of nations. The state, wrote Hegel, is "the Divine Idea as it exists on earth." What more can one say of his respect for the importance of the state? Who else in modern times has ever thought so well of the state as to call it God-like?

Every state is the expression of what Hegel called a national spirit. Spirit, Hegel explained, is the opposite of matter, but he also meant many more things by it. Spirit for him was sometimes conscious aim, sometimes freedom, more often something akin to thought. The essence of a nation, as of an individual, is its spirit. Only individuals are capable of consciousness, of course, but all the individual minds in a state share a spirit of unity.

Hegel saw civilization entirely in terms of a nation together with its people as embodying a national spirit. Every people has its peculiar genius. The essence of spirit, he wrote, is activity, and it is always the activity of a people having specially defined national characteristics, for instance a particular religious worship, particular customs, constitution and political forms; these influence the events which make up the national history.

Every nation lives the same sort of life as the individual; it goes through stages of *growth, flourishing, decline* and *death*. A nation is *growing* when it expands, as when for instance the English explored and conquered India and increased their commerce with the world. A nation is *flourishing* when it is engaged in realizing its objects and defends itself against external violence. Once it has accomplished its ends it subsides, and this marks the beginning of its *decline*. It can still accomplish much in peace and war, at home and abroad; but the supreme interest has vanished from its life. The mere continuance of what has now become a customary life is what brings on its natural death.

Each national spirit represents a moment in the development of the world spirit, and the interplay between national spirits represents the movement of history. There is only one historical line of states representing the unfolding of the idea of the state. Only the people of one state at a time can play a significant part in this development, and these are what Hegel called "the world-historical peoples." The rest serve as satellites or onlookers. They may have been of political importance at some time in the past or they may be so in the future, but meanwhile they do not count. World history is a theater in which one nation after another, but only one at a time, occupies stage center. Without opposition no state plays any important role. A nation, like an individual, passes from youth to manhood and from manhood to old age and retirement.

The conflict between nations, Hegel insisted, is inevitable. Nations are carried along on the wave of history, and in each epoch a particular nation is "the dominant people in world-history for this epoch." A nation cannot choose when it will be great, that is already decided for it by the forces of history, for "it is only once that it can make its hour strike."

The Three Stages of History

The human spirit, Hegel declared, separates itself from nature, but only in order to construct a "second nature," which is the state, that symbol of reason, that "actual God upon earth." Of those states which have existed, Hegel described three kinds, represented by three chronological ages. There was first the Asian stage, then the double Greco-Roman stage, and finally the European stage. In political form these three stages were represented by, first, despotism; second, democracy and aristocracy; and third, monarchy.

For Hegel human history began in Asia. In Asia he found both the geographical cradle and the political infancy of the race of man. There was no freedom in the political institutions of Asian nations; the Oriental knows nothing of freedom and the potentate can do as he wishes. "The Orientals have not attained the knowledge that spirit—Man *as such*—is free; and only because they do not know this, they are not free." Religion, morality, law and custom are not severally distinguished, while social life has hardened into the caste system.

China, Hegel insisted, represented the infantilism of the human race, evidenced in the patriarchal form of government, and even more in the language, which is written in pictorial characters rather than in an alphabet, and sounds, Hegel said, like baby-talk. (It never seems to have occurred to Hegel that German might have sounded like that to the Chinese.)

In India things were only a little better. Individuals there had begun to assert themselves, Hegel thought. But the Hindu temperament according to Hegel was still sunk in childish dreaming and make-believe. Hindu ideas were mystical, fantastic and extravagant. Even the bodies of Indians betrayed their childishness: Hindu men looked boyish, while the beauty of Hindu women was langorous, fragile and unearthly. In sum, Hindu nature was like the human spirit in a dream condition.

The second stage is a double one, and it took place in Greece and Rome, the adolescence of the human race and its maturity. "The consciousness of freedom first arose among the Greeks, and therefore they were free; but they, and the Romans likewise, knew only that *some* are free—not man as such." The political institutions of Greece, since they were aristocratic and democratic, represented to some degree the growth of freedom though general freedom is not yet a common possession. Greek spirituality was born "in the daylight of knowledge" and was "moderated and transfigured into free and joyous ethical life." That Greek freedom was incomplete, however, is shown by the existence of a slave class.

The second half of the second stage was represented for Hegel by the Roman Empire. The sterner Roman maturity made the idea of the nation supreme, and subjected the individual will to the common needs of growth and national security. The struggle between the "substantial insight" of the aristocrats and the "free personality" of the common people degenerated into a conflict between ruthless, self-seeking power and a corrupt rabble, in the end marking the complete destruction of all ethical life.

The third and final stage of history is represented by European, more specifically by German, national culture. Hegel had now set the stage for the final act in the drama of the human spirit. "The German nations, under the influence of Christianity, were the first to attain the consciousness that man, as man, is free: that it is the *freedom* of spirit which constitutes its essence." In German culture the spirit at last becomes fully conscious of its freedom and freely wills the identification of the individual with the true, the eternal and the universal, in a word with the German state. Europe, and especially Germany as the chief exponent of European culture, learned from Christianity the essential unity of the human and divine natures, with an opposition between this world and the next (Hegel loved opposites), and succeeded in bringing the two together in the modern world.

Hegel always divided everything into threes, but sometimes he went further and subdivided each of the three into three more. The German stage of history was the third in a minor movement which began with the Reformation, and was continued by the French Enlightenment as the second movement. Only in the German state are the individual and society fused together, so that what the individual wills is what the state commands. This, Hegel argued, is what we mean by perfect freedom.

We have noted in Hegel's account that "the history of the world travels from east to west, for Europe is absolutely the end of history." The last stage of history, he solemnly declared, is that of our own time. Hegel did not shrink from making dogmatic statements. It would have been fun to ask him what was to happen after Europe, and therefore history, came to an end.

In a much quoted epigram Hegel himself seems to have thought of that question, for he said that the lesson of history is that people have never learned anything from history. And no wonder, for it does not work quite in the way they have ordinarily supposed: ". . . in history an additional result is commonly produced by human actions beyond that which they aim at and obtain, that which they immediately recognize and desire. They gratify their own interest; but something further is thereby accomplished, latent in the actions in question, though not present to their consciousness and not included in their design."

The state for Hegel was supreme in every way. There can be no rules between states, no international law, for that would limit the power of the state which should have no limits. War, not peace, shows the health of the state, whose history is the march of spirit in the world and an unfolding of the order hidden within it. In this sense the state is wiser than any individual's understanding of it. It is the state which gives to all institutions their interdependence, and individuals participate in the state only indirectly, by being members of associations, guilds, estates and classes. Economics, politics, the legal system and the ethical philosophy, all link in a common submergence in the unity of the state.

In Hegel's day Germany was not unified. In fact it was the last of the European nations to become organized as a nation-state. Hegel, seeing the power of such a state when the French overran the land of Germany, in 1806 after the battle of Jena, wished for such power for his own country. The pendulum of thought and of events—they go together—always moves too far in each direction.

Hegel was not the only German to believe that nationalism should have no bounds, that there could be no such thing as an excess of nationalism. From having been the loosest of federations Germany became the most highly organized of western nations. Having permitted large individual freedoms, Germany swung all the way over to allowing no individual freedoms at all. It is a short distance from the thought of Hegel to the thought of Hitler, who was for a time able to put his thought into practice. He too believed that the individual should submerge himself in the life of the state, and the result, as we now know, was disastrous for Germany and to a large extent for much of the world.

World-Historical Individuals

It was to Hegel's credit that he saw the independence of history from the deliberate efforts of individuals. The movement of history is, so to speak, predetermined by historical forces, by the nature of that logic of opposition which runs through everything in the world, human and otherwise. There appear occasionally in history, however, outstanding individuals who in the course of pursuing purely personal goals manage to serve the larger social and cultural movements which activate states. This is what Hegel, in a famous phrase, has called "the cunning of reason."

"The particular is for the most part of too trifling value as compared with the general" but the general works through the particular. The *cunning of reason* lies in the fact that it sets the passions to work for it, while that which develops its existence pays a penalty and suffers loss. It is shown in its highest operation, Hegel explained, in the careers of such men as Alexander, Caesar and Napoleon. Such "world-historical individuals", in the very act of helping themselves, unintentionally do the business of moving the logic of history along destined paths.

The importance of world-historical individuals often escapes the notice of those around them. In what may have been intended as a sly autobiographical note, Hegel observed that even the high and the mighty have to eat and drink and make friends, and quoted a well-known proverb, "No man is a hero to his valet." It was Hegel's insight that added "not because the hero is no hero but because the valet really is a valet." Such a hero nevertheless is a force which may crush down many an innocent flower and destroy many an object in its path.

Every man is aware of his position in his business or profession, in his community and even in his country, but only the great man is aware of his place in history. History does not necessarily take immediate account of him; sometimes as in the case of Napoleon, it does, and sometimes as in the cases of Shakespeare and Marx, it does not. The great man is a guide for his times. He sees where things are going and leads everyone there.

World-historical individuals, then, have not always been entirely unaware of their role. Often they have sensed that they are being used by the Time-Spirit to further its ends, and have recognized that in the process they may have been destroying themselves. "If we look at the fate of these World-historical persons whose vocation it was to be the agents of the World-Spirit we shall find it to have been no happy one. They attained no calm enjoyment; their whole life was labor and trouble; their whole nature was nought else but their master-passion. When their object is attained they fall off like empty hulls from the kernel. They die early, like Alexander; they are murdered, like Caesar; transported to St. Helena, like Napoleon."

Hegel could not share his greatness with them, for he thought himself free and above the battle, as they were not. "The free man is not envious of them but gladly recognizes what is great and exalted, and rejoices that it exists."

Napoleon as a World-Historical Individual

The best example of what Hegel meant by a "world-historical individual" was Napoleon. Hegel mentioned him in this connection, but our strongest evidence comes from Napoleon himself. In the next three paragraphs I have put together some scattered sentences quoted from various places but all written by Napoleon. Only the arrangement is mine. Remember, then, that in what follows it is Napoleon himself who is speaking.

"The greater one is, the less free will one should have: one depends upon events and circumstances. I declare myself the most enslaved of men. My master has no pity; and by my master I mean the nature of things. I feel myself pushed toward an unknown goal. When I have reached it an atom will be enough to overwhelm me. I have never been master of my own movements; I have never really been entirely myself. I am not as other men are, and the laws of morality and convention cannot have been made for me. What man would not let himself be stabbed on the condition that he had been Caesar?

"Do you know what I admire most in the world? The impotence of force to organize anything. Imagination governs the world. In the harmony of universal comfort and well-being of which I was dreaming, in such a way Europe might soon have become a single nation, and any man, wherever he travelled, might have felt that he was in his native country all the time.

"What will history say? What will posterity think? Men, like pictures, must be seen in a favorable light. Our final ordeals are above all human forces."

These were Napoleon's own words. Surely I can say to my reader: you have just heard from a man who knew himself to be an instrument of destiny and a World-historical individual. Not all great men are aware of the part they are playing. Napoleon knew himself to have had the effect of a hurricane, and he did do much to sweep away the outmoded monarchies of Europe and thus leave the field free for the introduction of democracies. They were not slow in coming.

Hegel at His Best—and Worst

The one characteristic that marks off the genius from the mediocrity is that the genius is never middle-of-the-road. He is almost never fairly good. He does some things supremely well—better in fact than anyone else could do them—and other things badly. Hegel was a genius.

At his best Hegel had a penetrating vision. He saw that history really does work in terms of the interdependence of opposites and that there is a kind of logical progression to it. He saw also, and importantly, that while men think they manage their own affairs they really do not, and that nations often move in directions which none of the leaders or the people necessarily want to pursue. Cultures, civilizations if you like, lead lives of their own, directed by an inner necessity which no one yet quite understands.

Hegel saw clearly, and perhaps for the first time, the significance of the culture-hero, the "World-historical individual" who, known to himself or not, embodies the values of his culture to such an extent that they rise or fall with him; he is among the great ones whose footsteps shake the earth.

Germany was one of the last European countries to become a nation and Hegel never lived to see his dream of it come true. He died in 1831, still thinking that Germany would be unified under Austrian leadership. Thirty-six years later the North German Confederation was assembled, and adopted a constitution, with a centralized military system, under the command of the King of Prussia, with Bismarck as Chancellor. In 1870 Germany fought a war against France and won.

Hegel had learned from one of his masters, Fichte, to glorify war. Like all those who think well of wars as an instrument of national policy, Hegel had in mind of course winning them and would have been happy about the victory of 1870. But what about the crushing defeats of Germany in the two world wars that were to follow? The war policy ruined Germany.

It need not have been like that. Germany had at the time

paths to choose. At the turn of the century and for the next two decades the Germans excelled in the arts of peace. German science, German education, German scholarship, was the highest in Europe, or anywhere, for that matter. They could have conquered the world through the spread of culture, which would have helped everyone and harmed no one. Instead they took the Hegelian way of war, and destroyed themselves in the process.

Yet in some dim fashion Hegel understood that for all of Europe's triumphs he was witnessing the last decades of its domination. For he thought he understood European Civilization, and believed that one could understand something clearly only when it was on the road to decay. Minerva was the ancient Roman goddess of wisdom, and Hegel pointed out that Minerva's owl only begins its flight in the gathering dusk.

At his worst Hegel was merely foolish. What else can one say of such extreme nationalism? There is no doubt that he identified the ideal with Germany and saw the right only in terms of the triumph of force. To a large extent he was echoing the opinion of his fellow citizens; and therefore while it was foolishness it was at the same time dangerous foolishness, as subsequent events amply proved.

His opinions of other nationals were no less foolish. That the Chinese were childish, or that history would come to an end when Europe came to an end, could hardly be taken seriously as the opinions of a great philosopher; and yet they were.

Let me quote one of his typical predictions: "America has always shown itself physically and psychically powerless, and still shows itself so." This is certainly Hegel at his worst; the best that can be said on his behalf is that he never felt himself bound by the requirements of consistency. Some pages later, he added: "America is the land of the future, where, in the ages that lie before us, the burden of the world's history shall reveal itself." So history would not come to an end with Europe after all.

I have saved the worst for last. Hegel pointed out that the only essential connection between the Europeans of his day and the Negroes was that of slavery: "In this," he declared, "the Negroes see nothing unbecoming them." In fact, he added in support of this thesis, the English who have done the most to abolish the slave-trade are themselves treated by the Negroes as enemies. Since this passage speaks for itself, I leave it at that.

Chapter 8

Marx's Communism

At first sight it may seem strange to encounter a chapter on Karl Marx and communism in a book devoted to accounts of civilization, but Marxism is certainly one of the accounts. The ambition was to establish nothing less than a new civilization on the ashes, and over the dead bodies, of the old.

The most important of the founding fathers was Karl Marx. Marx was born in Trier in 1818. His father was a Jew converted to Protestantism, in which faith the young Karl was brought up. At the Universities of Bonn and Berlin, to meet his father's wish, he was enrolled in the Faculty of Law; but after the death of his father in 1838 he devoted himself to philosophy and history. He became interested in the Hegelian left through the influence of a circle of young teachers who, having begun with a loyalty to the Prussian state, at first opposed only organized religion, but then turned against the monarchy, and finally against the idea of the state itself.

After a time as editor of a radical newspaper, Marx was attracted to materialism and, through the influence of Engels and others, to communism. As a member of the Communist League

he joined with Engels in the writing of the Communist Manifes-
to which openly calls for social revolution. He tried working in
Belgium, France and Germany as a member of revolutionary
groups, but when these efforts failed he settled in London and to
a life of writing under conditions of poverty, supported by Friedrich Engels, whose father was a wealthy factory owner in
Manchester. He died in London in 1883.

Marx was a German political theorist who failed in his attempts to influence the labor unions in Germany and thereafter
spent his life in London writing his great three-volume work on
Capital in the British Museum Library. *Capital* and the books
he wrote with Engels, which together amount to a theory of civilization, were the moving force behind Lenin and the Russians
who made the revolution of 1919.

It is a fascinating story, especially the part about the life of V.
I. Lenin, who as an *emigré* was a poor pants-presser in New
York before the first world war, but who was run into Russia in
a sealed train during that war by the Germans who thought
that by starting a revolution there he would weaken the eastern
front and so take the pressure off the German army. Lenin also
added to the theory of communism by showing in principle how
it could be applied in practice, and he was followed after the
revolution by Josef Stalin, who ran the Russian state.

Communism, like Christianity, began as a revolutionary
movement conducted in the name of the masses who make up
the lowest economic class. If we substitute the name of Marx for
that of Jesus, and Lenin for St. Paul, we have a perfect parallel.
The doctrine that we now call communism for short (it has
many other more technical names) was the work of a small
group of men. Together they made a program which could be
followed anywhere. Indeed it has been followed, chiefly in Communist China, but also in some of the Balkan states (compelled
perhaps by the Russians), and in Cuba.

Our interest in it here of course is not a theory of politics
but as an explanation of the nature of civilization. It is a one-

cycle theory—and again it is not. Marx tried to account for civilization in a five-stage movement, where the fifth stage repeats the first but with notable changes, which suggests that the cycle may repeat. This part of the theory is somewhat vague, however, and we need not dwell on it.

Since Marx's theory of communism, on the one hand, and communism itself as practiced in the Soviet Union, on the other hand, are very far from being one and the same thing, it is best to present them separately. First, then, his theory.

The Five Stages

Marx's theory calls for five stages of development in the history of mankind. These are (1) primitive communism, (2) slavery, (3) feudalism, (4) capitalism, and (5) communism. The fifth stage has something in common with the first, as the names suggest, and is in a sense a return to the first stage but under more enlightened conditions. Both the first and fifth stages are of those societies in which there is public ownership of all property, but in the fifth stage there is a higher organization. Of these five, Marx marked out the last three for special attention.

According to Marx man arose biologically from the ape, but it was not the operation of evolution alone that was responsible for man. Work set him apart from the ape; by work man made himself, and by work he will continue to change and evolve. By his labor, acting on the external world and changing it, he also changes his own nature. In a word, labor created man. With labor came the gradual development of consciousness and speech, and eventually the appearance of the first societies.

Men were distinguished from the lower animals, in other words, when they begin to produce their own means of subsistence. This was their way of expressing their life. But production means not only *what* they produced but also *how* they produced it. The nature of man therefore depends upon the conditions under which he produces material goods. Marx's name for this is the economic relations of material production. These of course are social relations, and they are basic to human life, for they determine all other relations whether familial, political, national, legal or ideological.

The five stages in which all social and cultural history develops, according to Marx, are as follows.

(1) The earliest stage of social life was the "primitive communal" stage. There was no private ownership, not even of land. Life was nomadic and episodic, as represented for instance by the North American Plains Indians. The first primitive societies were classless societies in their most rudimentary form, but when man first began to emerge from this kind of primitive society, he found himself in a class society based on private property and the division of labor.

(2) The occurrence of slavery was connected with the invention of tools as instruments of production and the division of labor. Criminal codes came next, and the organizations to enforce the codes. In a class-structured society, the condition of "war of all against all" exists, and man is separated from other men, opposed to them and so fragmented in his existence. "Mankind always sets itself only such tasks as it can solve" and "the task itself arises only when the material conditions necessary for its solution already exist". "In broad outlines," Marx went on, "we can designate the Asiatic, the ancient, the feudal and the modern bourgeois modes of production as so many epochs in the progress of the economic formation of society."

(3) We have seen that social life began with a form of primitive communism, from which the slave-holding society developed. In the feudal society which came after the primitive communal society, serfs replaced slaves and hereditary landlords replaced slave-owners. The stage before capitalism, then, was feudalism; socialism was yet to be evolved.

Each stage in history is characterized by a typical method of producing and exchanging goods. Social inequality is economic, and so the source of servitude is not political. It lies rather in the division of labor which private ownership brings about, and in a system of production which permits one class to monopolize the means of production.

What Marx had proved, he thought, was that the existence of economic classes came as the result of particular phases in the development of the means of production, and that the appearance of economic classes leads inevitably to class struggle. What I did that was new, Marx wrote, was to prove that the existence of classes is bound up with particular phases in the mode of material production, that the class struggle necessarily leads to the dictatorship of the working class, and that this dictatorship is itself only a transition to the abolition of all classes and the establishment of a classless society.

(4) The class struggle has existed ever since there has been a division of labor, and the aim of the struggle has been to gain control of the means of production. Beginning with the feudal system, the first class struggle was that of the middle class against the landed aristocracy, and when the members of that class won they established the factory system of production and with it the economic system of capitalism.

The industrial revolution had created a class of large manufacturing capitalists, but also a class—and a far more numerous one—of manufacturing work people. The next stage, Marx was sure, would be the struggle of the workers against the dictatorship of the middle class, to gain control of the ownership of the means of production, that is to say, the ownership and hence the control of the factories (period of socialism).

(5) In a final stage, after a period of dictatorship of the working class, society would get rid of all classes and establish a classless society (attainment of communism). And since the Marxists believe that the state is always an instrument of oppression in the hands of the ruling class, a classless society would also be a stateless society, which we are told, would be not a condition of anarchy but of perfect order, a perfect society. The details of just

how this was to work out were left a little vague. Marx was more interested in getting the worker's revolution going than he was in concentrating on the remote future.

The class struggle over control of the means of production is what determines everything else, Marx claimed. It is responsible for the economic relations which dictate morality, religion, and philosophy, everything in fact in social life. The production and exchange of goods carry a particular system of law and politics as well as the so-called spiritual undertakings of civilization, such as the arts and the sciences. Political economy, Marx called the main theory and, after the fashion of his time, made a whole enterprise out of the various parts, and in this showed how they were welded together more intimately than had ever been shown before.

Feudalism in Marx's day had already given way to capitalism, which was shot through with contradictions that would generate its own downfall, he predicted. Impoverishment of workers and competition between capitalists would surely end in the collapse of capitalism. According to the labor theory of value, labor is always forced to produce more than it receives, and capital will accumulate in the hands of the masters, in fewer and fewer hands, until wealth becomes a matter of monopoly capital and the poverty of the many becomes more painfully obvious. The result can only be a revolutionary situation in which the factories will be seized by the workers and in this way the means of production socialized.

Marxist Theory, Russian Practice

Since Marx had been inspired by the new industrialism to construct his theory of civilization, he thought that the communist revolution would occur first in the most advanced of industrialized countries, England and Germany. It occurred instead in the most industrially backward of countries, Russia. The men who made the revolution there were led by Lenin, a unique combination of thinker and man of action, who wrote books to show how Marx's theory should be applied, and then applied it himself in the Russian Revolution of 1917.

Communism as a working government owes much to Lenin for both its theory and its practice. The movement has been regarded since his day as having followed the philosophy of Marx, Engels and Lenin. Lenin, responsible for the Party—understood as a working class elite distinct from the workers—insisted on absolute and inflexible obedience to it; and it was the Party that consolidated the political and economic gains effected by the Revolution.

When Lenin died in 1924 there was a power struggle between his two chief lieutenants, Josef Stalin and Leon Trotsky. When Stalin won Trotsky fled to Mexico, where he was later murdered by Stalin's agents.

The quarrel between Stalin and Trotsky involved not only a personal struggle for power but also a practical question of strategy. Stalin wanted communism secured first in a single country, Russia, so that it could not be overthrown and could later be used as a base for revolutionaries who were to fan out over the world. Trotsky's ideas were closer to those of Marx and Engels, who had called for a world revolution.

The result of Stalin's victory was to give communism a new turn. It became united with a nationalism as fierce as anything the old imperialists had ever contemplated. Many of the repressive methods of Czarist Russia were continued in the Soviet Union, for instance the practice of committing critics to mental hospitals—as though anyone who dared to differ with the authorities must be insane—has been continued under the government of Brezhnev just as it was under the government of Czar Alexander II. The foreign policy of the Russian leaders, whether the Czar's officials or the members of the Presidium of the Supreme Soviet, remains the same.

What has not been stressed sufficiently, then, is that the government of the Soviet Union both in its internal and external policy is not merely an application of Marx's communist theory, but also an extension of the tradition of the Imperial Russia of the Czars, which has cast a long shadow. This is exemplified by the conquest and domination of the Balkan states and of Poland, as well as by the continued opposition to China. And so far as internal policy is concerned, many of the same practices that were considered so hateful under the Czars are in effect today. Consider for example the widespread use of the secret police. The name has changed but the function remains the same, and citizens live in the same terror of them as they have always done. Obviously theory in politics is one thing and practice another. Marx had claimed that the state is an instrument of oppression in the hands of the ruling class, but if so it is not less true when the ruling class is a communist bureaucracy. The Marxist theory as applied in the Soviet Union by communists, led by Stalin and his successors, and in China by Mao-Tse-tung and his associates, bears more resemblance to the tyranny of the Czars in Russia and to the rule of the old war-lords in China than it does to any ideals of socialism. A political theory which was intended to end oppression and nationalism has been distorted to intensify them. Individual rights, freedoms, liberties, cherished and protected by law in the western democracies, have not existed in the communist bloc countries. Instead they have been subjected to rigid dictatorship.

On the other hand, what is not so obvious to observers is that the communists have raised the economic standard of living for the masses. It is not nearly as high as it is in western industrial democracies, but we must remember that before the revolution most Russians were serfs, illiterate, deprived of the benefits of civilization. Now they receive education, medical attention, and some of the consumer goods of which the people in the western countries are so enamoured. The communists have done much to improve their lot, and if the masses looked back to the conditions that prevailed before the Revolution that would be enough for them to defend the present government with all their power.

The Marxists, faithful to Hegel's movement of opposites, had said that the dictatorship of the capitalist class has to be followed by a period in which there is a dictatorship of the proletariat, of the working class, but that this would then lead to a classless society. When that day came, the state would "wither away" because it would no longer be needed.

Lenin, it is well known, took a more serious view of the ultimate goal of the "withering away of the state" before he gained power than after. The phrase remained an embarrassment to the regime until under Khrushchev it was revived. It represents the theory that services normally performed by the state would eventually be taken over by public and private social organizations. There is no evidence of this yet and nobody expects it soon.

As I write, the prediction made by Marx—that when communism triumphed wars would be abolished—seems to have failed. Europe had just experienced the bloody wars of 1830 and 1848, Marx was to see another one in 1870, and he declared that wars are the instruments by means of which the capitalists gain booty for themselves, but recent events have shown that war is by no means a monopoly of the capitalists. The Soviet Union invaded Hungary with tanks in 1956, and Czechoslovakia in 1968—both communist countries but not considered sufficiently subservient to the Russians. In the early seventies, the Russians were still maintaining two armored divisions in Czechoslovakia. And the competition between the Soviet Union and Communist China is still so intense that a war between them could break out at any time. The evidence seems to be, alas, that wars are human and not confined to any nation, class, or stage of development.

The English historian, Arnold Toynbee, has somewhere called communism "the holy atheistic Church militant." The communists have always proclaimed themselves atheists, not because they could prove that God does not exist—that seems as hard to prove as that He does—but because of Marx's observation that the Church is an instrument of oppression in the hands of the ruling class and that religion serves as "the opium of the masses."

Despite Marx's criticism of the utopian socialists, he too thought that the course of history and progress go hand in hand. So far, the accomplishments of the communists in Asia do not seem likely to outpace those of the industrialists and democrats in Europe and America, and Marx's thought, that capitalism would die of its own contradictions, might have been right had it remained as uncompromising as it seemed to him and indeed as it was in his day. But it did not.

Some of Marx's insights into capitalism were of course true. He saw that under capitalism industrial production is conducted in an orderly fashion but there is an anarchy of exchange and distribution. He was right in thinking that social historians have badly neglected the role of economics in human life. He was wrong, however, when he supposed that a state born in conflict and violence, methods which have been not only approved but encouraged, can ever take its place as a peaceful arrangement. He could hardly have seen that his philosophy would be used to justify a dictatorship so complete and so ruthless. He failed also to estimate the strength of capitalism under democracy; it has obtained new strength from its modifications. The middle class strengthened by the individual freedoms it sponsors has been able to produce the highest standard of living and the lowest death rate ever attained in a civilized society.

Above all, perhaps, Marx failed to predict the rise of the labor unions and the price that the capitalists have had to pay in taxes to stay in business. The condition of the working man is far from what it was in Marx's day and improving steadily. In the early seventies the American farmer was producing enough wheat to feed the Russians, and to help the Canadians to do the same for Communist China.

A lesson of history seems to be that the effect of a social revolution for the masses is the exchange of one set of masters for another. When Tolstoy wrote that the rich will do anything for the poor except get off their backs, he might have said the same thing for the powerful. The great French historian Jules Michelet, who discovered Vico's ideas in 1824, held that the common people are more important than their leaders, but there are few if any leaders who have ever acted as if they thought so.

A social revolution results sometimes in a gain, sometimes in a loss, more often in a mixture of the two. The Christian Revolution which came toward the end of the Roman Empire was responsible for a decay in social conditions, judged by the state of affairs which followed in the Middle Ages. On the other hand, the French Revolution of 1789 led eventually to a sharp rise in the standard of living of the middle classes made possible by capitalism, a standard which has since been extended to the working class in western industrial countries. The Russian Revolution of 1917 led to a considerable improvement in the living conditions of the masses in the Soviet Union but also, as we have seen, to the dictatorship of the Communist Party, so that another difference between Marxist theory and Russian practice is the development of a large bureaucratic class which needs to maintain itself in power. There are only a million party members out of more than two hundred and thirty million Russians, and it is the party members who run Russia. Many eyewitnesses have written books which show that the Party constitutes a new privileged class, a new aristocracy, even though that name is forbidden. There is nothing in Marx and Engels to justify such domination by an aristocracy. Finally, the absolute power of the handful of men who make up the Presidium of the Supreme Soviet, the ultimate ruling body in the Soviet Union, is what the "dictatorship of the working class" has finally come to represent.

These three—the Presidium of the Supreme Soviet, the bureaucracy and the secret police—hold absolute power in the Soviet Union; the Supreme Soviet dictates everything in the society, every move of the private citizen, and controls all the press, the arts, the literature, the sciences. Once again there is nothing in Marx and Engels to indicate that such rigid control should be exercised. Its apologists would say that this is what the dictatorship of the working class comes to, but what it actually comes to is the *control* of the working class as well. We have learned that after a period, the length of time left unspecified, the state is supposed to "wither away" because it will no longer be needed, but in the history of the world there is no record of any group, firmly in control of power in a society, that has voluntarily relinquished its control. As a matter of record, the entire conception of the classless society of the future is left vague. Marx was not specific; he was simply sure that in the classless society the institutions we have now would be changed, and that the changes would be fundamental. For example, the family would change, though he did not predict exactly how. Though women surrender to men for reasons of economic dependence, that reason would no longer exist, and sex relations would have to have a freer base, resting entirely on love. Marx turned aside all questions concerning the details of life in the coming classless society by saying that he refused to "write recipes for the cook shops of the future". It takes a different sort of philosophy to operate a society than it does to start one.

Is Communism a New Civilization?

At the present time two thirds of the world's population are living under some form of communism. In many of the countries besides Russia several generations have grown to maturity knowing nothing else. Controlled through education, the popular press, television, in fact all the mass media, to such an extent that they have no true idea of how different things are elsewhere in the world.

The question we must ask ourselves in looking at the shape of history is: Are the communists producing a new civilization or only continuing a variant of the older European Civilization? We know that much that makes up the communist societies came from older capitalist societies, from Marx and Engels themselves as well as much of European and American science and technology. The elements are European, but are the Russians doing anything entirely new with them? At first the answer to this question might have been yes; but it does not look that way any more. Shortly after the Revolution the idealists and do-gooders among us flocked to the Soviet Union (when they could get in), on the assumption that a paradise was about to be established on earth. No one would have to work hard, no one would have to go hungry, there would be liberty and justice for all—a dream that was soon shattered by the harsh realities. The cruelties and murders perpetrated by the government under the rule of Stalin are now well known; nobody can fool himself about that paradise any longer. The reign of terror has been relaxed somewhat, but the terror continues, a very real thing for dissidents and even for mild critics of Soviet policy and practice. Exit visas are prized documents, obtainable, except in rare cases, only by those whose conformity can be relied on absolutely. How long this situation will be continued, whether it will be relaxed when the present generation of bureaucrats dies and another takes its place, cannot be predicted with any degree of accuracy; there are too many variables in every social situation. Things will change—they always do—but in what direction is difficult if not impossible to say.

It can hardly be denied that the Russians subscribe to the aims of international communism and are bent on world conquest. Despite severities and scarcities, bound to occur in a country when it is trying to shift from an agricultural to a scientific-industrial economy, so large a proportion of available funds and energy is devoted to building a military machine that it staggers the imagination. Between the Russians and their goal stand two other giants, Communist China and the United

States, and perhaps the outcome will be different from what anyone may think now, and all three will be supplanted. Only a hundred years ago it looked as though the issue of world domination would be decided in the struggle between Germany, France and England, all three of whom have been reduced to second-rate powers. Are we looking now at second-rate powers of a hundred years in the future? It is certainly possible.

The aims of men shift from time to time in ways that are not perfectly understood. Only too often the pleasures of this world have been surrendered in exchange for those presumed to come in a life after death. The Egyptian Civilization was constructed on such a promise, and so was the Christian Civilization of the Middle Ages in Europe. Civilizations sometimes seem to be one-dimensional, devoted to the pursuit of a single goal. It does not take great imagination to picture a future civilization in which no one will be much interested in consumer goods, in radios and washing-machines, and the like. Both capitalism and its foster-child, Asian communism, are rightly based on the assumption that everyone now is so interested. What the Russians want most in the world is a stream of consumer goods comparable to that of the United States. But there may come a day when what men pursue most eagerly is not a motor car or a television set but something else, something not listed now in our catalogue of goods. When such a day comes what will society and its government be like?

For the time being I should have to insist that communism is not a new civilization but only a new approach to European Civilization, one that has succeeded in bringing a backward people into the twentieth century faster than could have been done in any other way. Civilizations are the products of men of genius who have had the freedom to operate in their own independent way, sometimes in a free society, but at other times in tiny corners possible to them in otherwise repressive societies. These men of genius have had not only the originality but also the energy to make new things that had not been in the world before. So Homer, Plato, Shakespeare, Mozart, and in our own country in our own time so Whitman, so Charlie Chaplin, Frank Lloyd Wright.

Now I see on the horizon in the Soviet Union nothing like them but only a desert of official standards, of mediocre convention, and of rigid conformity, in which nothing original or rebellious can bloom. I should make the same judgment of the tired old propaganda which is no more art than the acrobatic dance to dreadfully conventional music in the films exported by Communist China. If there is anything of genuine innovative value and fresh originality issuing from the two major communist powers, it is superbly well hidden.

Chapter 9

Danilevsky's Russia and Europe

Nicolai Danilevsky, the first of the modern students of civilizations, was born in 1822. He attended the University of St. Petersburg from 1843 to 1847 and took his M.S. in botany in 1848-49. Together with Dostoyevsky, he was arrested in 1849 in connection with the radical activities of the Patrashevsky Circle, and was imprisoned for one hundred days, which he spent reading *Don Quixote* in a French translation. Unlike Dostoyevsky, Danilevsky was acquitted. He was soon appointed to the staff of the governor of Vologda, and thereafter held a succession of governmental posts, as an economist, as an engineer in the Ministry of Agriculture, and as a special governmental representative on various committees. In 1852 he married the widow of a general; when in the following year she died of cholera he was grief stricken and did not marry again for almost a decade. In 1861 he married again and this time had five children.

His chief position was as a specialist in fisheries and he finally became the head of the Russian Commission on Fisheries. His first assignment as a fisheries statistician to the Volga River and the Caspian Sea, lasted from 1853 to 1857; later assignments took him to the Arctic, to Norway, and as far east as Prussia. He disliked city life, in 1867 bought a country estate in the Crimea, and his career lasted for the greater part of his productive life, from 1853 until his death in 1885.

His chief work, *Russia and Europe*, which he began to write in 1865 was finished in 1868 and first published in a journal in 1869. In 1880-81 he paid a visit to the south of France and to Switzerland, began some four years later to suffer intermittent heart attacks and in November of 1885 had a fatal one.

The Ten Great Civilizations

Danilevsky thought that there had been ten great "historico-cultural" civilizations in the world: the Egyptian, Semitic, Chinese, Hindu, Iranian, Hebrew, Greek, Roman, Arabian, and the European. Under the Semitic he included the ancient civilizations of Assyria, Babylonia, Phoenicia and Chaldea. Under the European he included what he called the Germano-Romanic. He recognized also two civilizations in the new world, the Mexican and the Peruvian, both of which met early and violent deaths at the hands of the European invaders.

There were two other historical types. Just as the great civilizations have been positive, so the second kind was of a negative, destructive type: peoples and tribes whose function it was to bring to an end senile and dying civilizations. Examples of destructive peoples who put to death "decrepit civilizations which were lingering in their death-agony" were the Mongols, the Huns and the Turks.

The third kind Danilevsky described as "ethnographic material," a sort of grab bag containing tribes that serve as mere material for the construction of the others, non-historical peoples, the remnants of past civilizations. A good example of such neutral peoples, who furnish the human raw materials to civilizations, were the Finnish tribes; and some historico-cultural peoples are reduced to this state after their prime is past, for instance the Romans after A.D. 476.

Most of these civilizations were what Danilevsky described as "transmittable" types, civilizations capable of passing on their achievements to other civilizations, but a few were "solitary" types which could not: he gave as examples the Chinese and Indian civilizations. This difference accounts, he thought, for what Europeans and Americans described in Danilevsky's day as Western progress and Oriental stagnation.

Every great civilization according to Danilevsky goes through the same life cycle as any other organism, for each the same account of its life-history can be given—stages of birth, growth, flourishing, decline and death—and this basic similarity is what supports the idea of a science of history; but the basic differences also must be taken into account. Every civilization develops its characteristic form, its rare and matchless values, and adds in this way to the total volume of human culture. Then each passes away, with its unique pattern, which will not be continued in the same way by any later civilization. Thus, like individuals, every civilization is at once a member of the same species and to some extent unique. The chief divisions of history must be made therefore in terms of the great civilizations.

Danilevsky saved what he thought was best for last. The Slavic peoples, he said, represented chiefly by Russia, were in process of becoming the eleventh great historico-cultural civilization. Russia according to Danilevsky had not participated either in European evil or in European good. She had not gone through feudalism and chivalry, had not experienced either Catholicism or Protestantism, had not suffered the period of oppression of scholasticism in the Middle Ages, but then neither had she enjoyed the freedom of thought that brought modern science to birth. We must remember that when Danilevsky was saying this in a book first published in 1871, the Russian Revolution of 1919 had of course not yet occurred; Russia was what somebody had described as a "sleeping giant." Danilevsky made a great thing of the repeated rejection of Russia by Europe. He mentioned the invasions of Russia by Europeans but had nothing to say about the occasional invasions of Europe by Russians. What he proposed in his book was the rejection by Russia of European Civilization: what Europe offered Russia was the task of spreading European Civilization in the East, primarily in Central Asia, but Russia had better things to do than to serve as a transmission-belt for European Civilization to Central Asians.

The Development of Civilizations

Humanity has a creative mission, and the civilizations are the main vehicles by which it is accomplished. Every civilization develops its own patterns in the fine arts, in the sciences, in philosophy and in all other creative enterprises. But each civilization develops only one of the great creative values; none has developed them all. Danilevsky gave us some examples: the Greek civilization strongly emphasized *beauty*, more in fact than has been done in any other civilization; the Roman genius went into *law* and *political organization*; the European specialty has been *science*; the Chinese contributed the ideal of the *practically useful*; the Indian creativity focused on *imagination* and *mysticism*.

The idea of "progress" in history is absurd, Danilevsky insisted. Each civilization produces something of its own, which may be greater than what another civilization produces of the same kind later. In literature, with the possible exception of Shakespeare, Europe has offered nothing to rival the Homeric epics or the tragedies of Aeschylus. Semitic (Hebrew) Civilization was supreme in religion, the Roman in law. No one would rank the German philosopher, Kant, above the Greek philosopher, Plato, nor the Italian sculpture of Canova above the Greek sculpture of Phidias.

Not only are the arts and the humanistic disciplines stamped with the peculiar characteristics of a civilization but so also are the sciences and technology, which are supposed to be the same everywhere. Each civilization leans toward some one of the sciences rather than the others, which is why the Greeks had a preference for geometry over the analytic method in mathematics: it was closer to the idea of beauty. Even science which is supposed to be international in fact is not. The French do mathematics better than anybody else, while the English excel in geology.

Danilevsky came very close to showing the importance of philosophy as the key to a civilization when he talked about the way in which the basic theories of the philosopher, Thomas Hobbes, the economist, Adam Smith, and the biologist, Charles Darwin, together displayed the central trait which was native to the English. It is not hard to find common ground, Danilevsky wrote, between Hobbes's theory that the natural condition of man involves a state of war of all against all, Smith's theory that free economic competition is natural and has its own laws, and Darwin's theory that all organisms are engaged in a struggle for existence. The English, he declared, have entered upon the "slippery slopes" of democracy. They were perhaps saved when their most radical element, the Puritans, emigrated.

When the English monopoly of world trade comes to an end, the English will face crises resulting from the tension between democratic tendencies and aristocratic structure. (That sounds remarkably like an analysis of contemporary England. How prophetic!) By way of contrast it is interesting to look at the attitude toward politics of the Russians who, Danilevsky declared, do not regard political authority as something hostile; they treat it with perfect trust and confidence. (Again prophetic.)

In the development of civilizations there is some overlapping, for not all separate movements proceed at the same pace. Danilevsky described this as *"lead"* and *"lag."* Political unification, for instance, may have preceded the period of blossoming in the same civilization, while the advances in the fine arts usually do precede those in the experimental sciences in every civilization. The period of decline starts earlier than is usually manifest.

The Five Laws of Explanation

There are according to Danilevsky five laws which account for the changes in the historico-cultural types of civilizations. I will state them first and then discuss them in his terms.

1. Every social group or family of peoples which is distinguishable by its language and capable of historical development constitutes a historico-cultural type.

2. If a civilization is to take root and grow, it must have political independence.

3. One civilization cannot transmit its basic principles to another. Each creates its own, under more or less influence from its predecessors or contemporaries.

4. For richness and variety of development there must be a federation of diverse racial groups within a given historico-cultural type.

5. Civilizations are like those plants we call hardy perennials whose growth period lasts indefinitely but with only one relatively short period of flowering and fruit-bearing which exhausts them once and for all.

A few comments on these laws as Danilevsky saw them and as we see them:

1. He placed great emphasis on language, and in this he was very much in anticipation of current thought. He classified peoples by their languages and, although he insisted on the greatness of the Slav peoples, he also claimed that the "qualitative difference between the races of man entirely disappear from view."

There is no doubt of course of the importance of language. We tend to make a cultural identification of a people by the language they speak; especially a language which has been in common use for a very long time tends to carry all sorts of values with it. The only criticism—and it is a serious one—is that there are other factors in civilization besides languages which count equally in importance. What are called artifacts, the material constructions which are intended to help in reducing human needs, should certainly also be counted: as we noted in Chapter 2, everything made in a society, from aspirin to automobiles, from books to buildings, from cheese knives to Chopin's piano compositions. Danilevsky thought of the languages people speak but he forgot the significance of some of the things they speak about.

2. The second law, he explained, accounts for why the Slavs developed a great civilization while the Celts, who were conquered by the Romans, did not; their development was brought to a sudden end and they lost their political independence at an early stage. The decline of Greek Civilization began when the Greeks were conquered, first by the Macedonians and later by the Romans.

3. Examples abound of the attempt to transpose a culture from one civilization to another. Alexander the Great failed to impose Greek Civilization upon the ancient Persians even though he conquered them, and witnessed a similar failure in our own day when the English endeavored to transmit their European Civilization to the peoples of India. India remains Hindu and not European.

4. This is a very important law and it goes dead against racism. That most civilizations do take their start when a conquering people mixes with the conquered tribes has certainly been true of European Civilization. The English, for instance, are a mixture of the native population with the Vikings, the Normans and many others—a mixture that worked very well. I can think of exceptions, however, where from a mixture no high civilization resulted: The Spanish conquerors mixed with the Indian populations of Central and South America without producing an outstanding civilization.

5. The flowering period of a civilization lasts on an average of four hundred to six hundred years, Danilevsky believed. This is in contrast with the life-span of a civilization, which can run for thousands of years. The period of decay and disintegration, however, begins so shortly after the period of flowering that it is almost contemporary with it. No one understands the aging of civilizations any more than what causes aging in the human organism.

The Coming Slavic Civilization

In writing his books, particularly *Russia and Europe*, Danilevsky had two purposes. Our interest in him here rests on the many insights in his comparative study of civilizations, a study which, with the exception of Ibn Khaldûn's work, was the first in the field and an immense influence on such later thinkers as Oswald Spengler and Arnold Toynbee. But his other purpose was the promotion of the importance of Slav Civilization.

By the term "Slav" Danilevsky referred to an ethnic group which included, among others, all those peoples to be found in eastern and southeastern Europe, the Russians, the Bulgarians, Serbo-Croats, Slovenians, Moravians, Czechs and Poles. We recall that every great civilization has its speciality, some field in which its creative power is supreme? Well, Danilevsky predicted that the creative power of the Slav civilization would lie someday in the building of a social and economic order—a social order based on economic elements.

Because of the proximity of the Slav peoples to those of Europe, a comparison of their stages of civilization is helpful. Danilevsky believed that in his day European Civilization had already entered upon its period of decline, while Slavic Civilization was on the threshold of its most creative period of flowering. That is pretty good predicting when you consider that Danilevsky, writing 58 years before the Russian Revolution, could not possibly have foreseen the establishment of a Marxist state.

Russia Versus Europe

European Civilization was five hundred years older than the Slavic, according to Danilevsky's estimates. The European was coming to the end of its period of flowering when the Slavic Civilization was just moving from its second stage to that of its maximum flowering. The decline of Europe had already begun in the seventeenth century, its creativity weakening and its cynicism increasing, but its lust for world domination growing. The success of a single world power could put an end forever to mankind's creative mission, which requires change and development.

Because of the vast differences between Slavic and European Civilizations, Danilevsky insisted, they could never understand each other or hope to. That is also why neither has been successful in interfering in the other's internal affairs. Poland in trying to become Europeanized only succeeded in losing the Slavic values and gaining a distorted and unbalanced "mongrel" culture. For this reason there can be no friendship between the aging European and the youthful Slavic Civilizations. There was more sympathy, Danilevsky thought, between the Russians and Americans than between the Russians and Europeans. Every people is what Danilevsky called "a spiritual organism." There is such a thing as a "national individuality," he claimed, and in the United States he saw the development of a new nationality, wholly different from that of the English. Europe, in a word, cannot help hating Russia, and so war between them is inevitable—a long-range prediction. For the present Danilevsky saw a kind of stand-off, a balanced co-existence between European, American and Slavic Civilizations. But for the present only the united Slavic Civilization was capable of fighting the European world-domination and so alone could guarantee the preservation of world equilibrium.

The antagonism, Danilevsky thought, cut very deep, and he devoted quite a few pages to discussing it, looking at it, of course, from the perspective of the Russia of his day, seeing on the one

hand a generous Russia trying to help Europe, and on the other
an ungrateful Europe. Though Russia had been no threat to
Europe Europe had been a threat to Russia, having forced her
to defend herself many times. Europe had always thought of
Russia as a dark force opposed to freedom, but to fight the invasion of Napoleon in 1812 was to oppose not freedom but
rather despotism. Why did Europe go to war with Russia in
1854 when all Russia had done was to attack the despotism of
Turkey? That same Europe stood by ten years later when Prussia and Austria had made war on liberal Denmark. The basis of
antagonism, Danilevsky thought, was the unfathomed depths of
tribal sympathies which by a sort of historical instinct lead people toward a goal unknown even to themselves.

That same kind of historical instinct accounted for the hatred
of Europe for Russia, neither of which could be explained merely
as a geographical area. They are two separate, distinctly different historico-cultural civilizations which happen to occupy ad-
joining lands. Russia never did form part of Europe, never participated in the truly European Holy Roman Empire of
Charlemagne; and her history has been different, peculiarly her
own. Danilevsky's intention was to turn Russia away from
Europe. Peter the Great had sought to introduce European influences, but Danilevsky believed that Russia should cultivate a
civilization of her own and not look to Europe, and accordingly
he pointed out that Russia was younger and had more of a future in developing a Slav Civilization than it did in following a
declining European one.

Finally, Danilevsky saw civilization in nationalistic terms.
When he called for a Slavic Civilization what he meant was a
Russian Civilization. All Slavs, he declared, should form a loo-
sely-knit federation "under the leadership of the united Russian
state." There were 80 million Russians, more of a population
than in any other Slav state, and so Russia would be the natural
leader of the Slavs. Then there could develop an independent
and autonomous Slavic Civilization, to include of course all the
Slavs but also some non-Slavic peoples: Greeks, Rumanians and

Hungarians. It should have its capital in Constantinople, which it would rename "Tsargrad" (Imperial City). The common struggle against Europe would make Russian the language of all the Slavs.

Russia, as a matter of fact, would be the proper leader, Danilevsky assured his readers, because the Russians are politically-gifted. They would introduce a greater measure of freedom and have less inclination to abuse it than other people; they are obedient, they respect and trust political authority, and do not meddle where they lack competence. For these reasons, he said, Russia has never had, and probably never will have, a political revolution!

Finally, after this Panslavic Union under the leadership of Russia becomes an accomplished fact, there should be a war with Europe, and especially with France, Europe's principal leader. Russia has no reason to attack India, but in a war with England India would be Russia's only defense. (Danilevsky was writing of course before the English had left India.) He compared the organization of war with Europe on the part of all the Slavs with the organization of Europe under the Pope during the Crusades.

Danilevsky: For and Against

There is much to be said for Danilevsky's accomplishment. He had probably never heard of Ibn Khaldûn, and so he was responsible for introducing the comparative study of civilizations into the western world. Many of his ideas were used by later workers in the field, particularly, as we shall see, by Spengler and Toynbee. To be the first in a new area of investigation is no means achievement, and Danilevsky's insights are often very acute and penetrating. He saw for example that civilizations do not move forward equally on all fronts but specialize in some one discipline.

In the end, however, he was an apologist for Russian nationalism, and this hot prejudice became the foreground for everything he had to say. What ought to distinguish the thinker who wishes to make all the civilizations his object of study is the absence of a private preserve which he finds superior and defends at all costs.

Unfortunately, Danilevsky did have one. He was against world conquest and world domination when it looked as though the British Empire might accomplish that goal, but he did not mind it at all when he thought that it might fall to the lot of the Russians. In fact he predicted just that: a Panslavic Union under the leadership of the Russians because they were the most numerous of the Slav states and the most politically gifted. This weakness, this broad inconsistency, does cancel much of the permanent value of Danilevsky's work as a contribution to a science of history, which is after all what he thought he was starting. However, no social science, history included, could make a scientific claim and yet have so special a case to plead, and in the end we must face him down for it.

Chapter *10*

Spengler's Decline of the West

The first man to gain considerable attention for his study of civilization was Oswald Spengler. His *Decline of the West* was a best-seller in every European country, and especially in the United States, where, when it was first published in two large volumes in 1926, it was widely read and even more widely discussed, for as the title indicates it predicted the decline of European and American Civilization. The prosperity of those years insured the disbelief of his readers, but they found his argument engaging nonetheless.

Spengler was born in Blakenburg, Germany in May 1880. He studied mathematics, biology, history and art at three universities: Halle, Munich and Berlin, then settled down to teach high school, first at Düsseldorf and later at Hamburg and Munich. He wrote the first draft of his book in the three years just prior to world war I, but the war prevented its publication. He rewrote the manuscript, it was first published in 1918, and was an instant success, selling some 90,000 copies in Germany alone.

How much was Spengler acquainted with the work of his

predecessors? The answer probably is, not very much. Certainly he knew nothing about Ibn Khaldûn, and probably did not even have any knowledge of the existence of his great book; he does not mention Vico and probably had not read him; there is some evidence that he did know about Danilevsky but had not read him in any detail. According to at least one student, H. Stuart Hughes, probably the best that Spengler could boast was a kind of second-hand knowledge of the general outlines of Danilevsky's study. Nevertheless, his work bears a strong resemblance to that of Danilevsky, as we shall see; though he credited only Goethe and Nietzsche as his principal influences, Goethe for his method and Nietzsche for the questioning faculty. From Goethe he learned to view social phenomena as wholes and to look for their overall pattern but not to employ the method of analysis— instead there was the penetrating method of intuitive contemplation. From Nietzsche he learned to value the will-to-power as the driving force behind all human activity, and he learned also about the "eternal recurrence" which he applied to civilization.

Civilizations as Living Organisms

Spengler thought that he had found the clue to the pattern of history when he considered civilizations as giant organisms; this comparison runs all through his most important work. All civilizations have the same life-cycle, which can most conveniently be divided into four periods, and to these Spengler gave the names of the four seasons.

In its spring a civilization has its birth and early childhood (Spengler called it a "culture" at this stage); in its summer it grows like a youth, in its autumn it comes to ripe manhood, and finally in its winter, having reached full civilization, it declines and dies of old age. These four seasons of a culture together last about a thousand years.

Cultures (or civilizations, it comes to the same thing) are organisms, and "world-history is their collective biography." All go through the same four stages in their development and, as we shall presently see, all exhibit the same characteristics at about the same period in their life-cycles. They are no different in this regard from a man or a tree. Spengler distinguished the idea of a culture from its material expression in practice, as one might distinguish, he said, a human soul from its body. There is a pattern to cultures or civilizations which admits of no variation. For every single person or event of any magnitude occurring in one culture, there is the corresponding person or event in every other In this sense, for instance, Alexander the Great (356-323 B.C.) and Napoleon (1834-1916) were "contemporaries." There are characteristic developments in cultures, or perhaps it would be better to say more broadly, the main outline of a culture, its inner structure, corresponds exactly to the inner structure of each of the others.

Each culture is a "superlative human organism" with its own distinctive life-style. The goal of each is the material expression of its peculiar personality in the form which makes up a complete culture-organism. Spengler was a little short on definitions, but then he was scornful of them. His name for this internal motivation is its "Destiny-idea," and we are supposed to learn in other ways what the word, Destiny, means. "Destiny is a word whose content one *feels*," it is what operates in history.

He often refers to particular cultures by dramatic names: the Classic Culture of ancient Greece and Rome is often called the Apollonian, after the God Apollo, as was Nietzsche's practice. The Arabic Culture Spengler named "Magian" after the Magi, who were said to be the wise men of the East according to Zoroaster. And Western Culture was called "Faustian" after the character of Faust in Goethe's play.

Danilevsky recognized ten great civilizations, Spengler only eight: the Egyptian, Babylonian, Indian, Chinese, Classical (or Greco-Roman), Arabian, Mexican and Western. Spengler preferred to call them cultures. He himself had a working knowledge of only two of the eight. Most of his many examples come from the Classical and the Western Cultures. All passed through their high periods and are either dead or in their last phase as civilizations.

Spengler did not think in abstract ideas, he preferred symbols. Reason employs signs, but symbols are signs which imply qualities and often even suggest forces. He did not have Aristotle's conception of man as a rational animal but instead thought of him as a user of symbols. He saw that men are moved more by feelings and emotions that they do not understand than by ideas that they do. Now the principal difference in the response to an idea from that to a symbol is that the response to an idea is intellectual whereas to a symbol it is emotional. Spengler did not rely upon reason and logic but rather on feeling and intuition, and history was to be interpreted, therefore, in terms of a universal symbolism. Among symbols, of course, some are more important than others. Every great culture, Spengler wrote, has its "prime symbol." This symbol differs from culture to culture, and is what each culture chooses when it awakens to its own self-consciousness *as* a culture on its own land. The prime symbol determines everything in the culture: its arts and sciences, its philosophy, its ways of thinking and believing, of living and acting.

The false idea that mathematics is the same for every culture, or that psychology is, must be given up; mathematics and psychology, like every other enterprise, differ from culture to culture. All the activities both internal and external of the individual are parts of the culture and inseparable from it. There is no such thing as science pure and simple; it would always be necessary to ask *whose* science: Western science, Arabic, Indian?

We may now look at some of Spengler's examples of these prime symbols and how they operate.

The prime symbol of Greco-Roman Culture is the sensuously presented perfect human body, nude statues ideally done. For Egyptian Culture Spengler recognized stone as the prime symbol. Eternal vaulted space, "the cavern feeling," is the prime symbol of Magian Culture, and under "Magian" Spengler included Arabic, Iranian, Islamic, Syrian and Jewish, everything in fact in the Middle East. Nirvana, the eternity of nothingness of the Hindu religion, is the prime symbol of Indian Culture. Pure and limitless space, he said, is the prime symbol of Western Culture.

Although he professed to find his symbolism extended into every corner of the civilizations he examined, you have only to look at his examples in order to see that for the most part they came from the characteristics of those works of art that showed peculiarities. For the Greco-Roman, or Classic Culture, Spengler had in mind the magnificent and idealized sculptures of men and women we have left from the hands of Phidias and other fifth-century geniuses. If he found that stone was the prime symbol of Egyptian Culture it was because most of the remaining monuments in Egypt consist of stone antiquities. The vaulted space of Magian Culture came from architecture also: the dome, the cupola, the barrel-vaulting and rib-vaulting of oriental mosques and other buildings.

India is a religious country, long under the influence of Hinduism; it was only natural, then, that Spengler should single out for special attention its conception of the after-life. In the culture of ancient Greece, Spengler noted that history as an account of the remote past hardly existed. All that counted for the Greeks was the present; they believed they were living in the most important time. Only Western Civilization is "historical" in the full sense of the term, that is to say, one which looks both into the remote past and the remote future, and conceives of endless space, therefore also of endless time. Spengler credited also as a prime symbol the clock, invented in the West, dread symbol of the flow of time.

It is characteristic of Western Civilization (that is to say, our own) to be able to look ahead, chiefly because, you recall, Western Civilization, unlike the Classical Civilization, has a highly developed time sense. The prophetic summing up of our own Civilization, which is the work of men like Spengler himself, is perhaps its most comprehensive conclusion. History reaches its highest point in the work of its greatest historian.

The Four Stages of Culture and Civilization

Spengler gave extensive descriptions of each of the four stages, three of culture and a fourth of civilization. We may now have a look at each of them in turn:

First perhaps it should be noted that history as such began with the first of Spengler's culture stages, the spring-time. Before that there was no history. Man was little more than an animal, a beast of prey roaming the earth. When he did settle down it was only to become rooted to the soil, a peasant who had no history; his village was not a part of world-history; he was what is eternal and independent of every culture; but to say this is to say that he was hardly human. In this pre-history stage there were no politics, no classes, no masses, no state, only blood-related tribes with their chiefs and their "proto-mystic soul," serving as a sort of social material for outsiders.

Such a pre-history stage preceded the beginning of every great culture. Spengler dated it for a few cultures: for the Greco-Roman Culture, it was the Mycaenean Age, the Age of Homer, about 1600 to 1100 B.C., for Western Culture it was from 500 to 900 A.D., the period which included the life of Charlemagne.

How do the high cultures originate? To this question Spengler made two answers. The first was that the question is wrong because, Spengler said, it assumes a cause-and-effect explanation, and causal conceptions are applicable only to the World-as-Nature; they amount to little more than an outrage, an unfortunate blunder when applied to the World-as-History.

His second answer was that the origin of any new living form, whether plant, animal, or human culture, is essentially a mystery. It appears suddenly, all at once in a definite shape, like a biological mutation from a lower form, and there is no rational or factual explanation of it. All that can be said is that the Destiny-course of these cultures is known to us only through the instinctive and intuitive historical logic of Destiny. In the case of the relations between a high culture and what went on before, we will find if we look, said Spengler, only the most thin and superficial of connections.

The period of spring-time is the awakening of the religious consciousness, "god-feeling" and "world-longing." "A culture is born in the moment when a great soul awakens out of the proto-spirituality of ever-childish humanity and detaches itself, a form from the formless. . . . It blooms on the soil of an exactly-definable landscape, to which plantwise it remains bound." This is the poetic age, the age of myth. It has its own typical kind of architecture, such as the pyramids of Egypt and the Gothic cathedrals of Europe.

Summer-time is the period of the critical spirit and of religious reformations such as that of Dionysus in the Classical Culture and Luther and Calvin in the Western Culture. Philosophy now puts in an appearance; this is the time for the Ionian nature philosophers like Thales, and the Eleatics like Parmenides, in Classical Culture; and for such men as Descartes and Leibniz in the Western Culture. It is also the feudal period when vassals and feudal lords struggle with one another or both with an overlord, when life is largely agricultural, when the castle appears in the countryside. At a later stage of this early period there emerges the aristocratic state, and the role of the city increases. Particular art forms also appear; the Ionic style in Greece, Moorish architecture in the Magian Culture—and it is the time when cities begin to be developed.

In the autumn phase culture for the first time reaches full maturity. There is an "Age of Enlightenment"; the height of intellectual creativity is reached; reason is now enthroned, and everything, including religion, is looked at rationally. But it is a period when culture is "more virile, austere, controlled, . . . assured of its sense of its own power," the time of the Early Middle Kingdom of Egypt, in Athens of the Pisistratidae, in Rome the age of Justinian, and in Europe of the Counter-Reformation. In Classical Culture, it is the period of Plato and Aristotle, in India that of the systematic development of Buddhism. It is the period in the Western Culture which produced Kant and Hegel. In the Magian Culture, the two leading philosophers, Alfarabi and Avicenna appeared.

"Every culture has its own civilization," Spengler wrote; indeed "the civilization is the inevitable destiny of the culture." It is the sequel but it is also the end. Civilizations may be external to the spirit of cultures but they are also the highest development of which the human species is capable.

The winter-time of culture is also the time of the great civilization phase, the time of the great cities and of the great empires. Formless masses of people congregate in the great cities without any bonds to hold them together, each friendless and not knowing his next-door neighbor. Religious belief declines; philosophy is altogether given over to skeptical thought; there is a general spirit of disillusionment, a world-weariness, a materialistic outlook which fosters "the cult of science, utility and prosperity."

The political form of the age begins by being democratic but ends with some form of Caesarism and imperialism. Caesarism, said Spengler, replaces money with naked force, and capitalism with socialism. World-history is the court which always decides in favor of the stronger, in this case the master-will. This is when the culture, as civilization, is at the very end of its life-cycle.

Spengler paid special attention to the fourth and last phase of culture, its civilization phase, when it is declining into death, because he thought that this was the phase in which our own Western Civilization now was. But he had an interesting theory of why a culture dies. "It dies when its soul has actualized the full sum of its possibilities in the shape of peoples, languages, dogmas, arts, states, sciences." Every culture strives like an artist to express in external material form what is contained within it, and when it has accomplished that and there is no more to do it comes to an end. The end of a civilization, however, does not necessarily mean its total obliteration. It may congeal and harden, it may mortify, and in this shape stand for hundreds or thousands of years, "like a worn-out giant of the primeval forest," thrusting "its decaying branches towards the sky."

One of Spengler's most interesting claims is that, when every great civilization is nearing its end, there appears what he called a "second religiosity," when the masses are weary and disillusioned, uncertain and insecure, tired and no longer creative, looking for salvation in a new kind of religious movement. It may be a revival of an old, abandoned religion or it may be a new one entirely, but usually it involves a heavy burden of mysticism. Theosophy, astrology, cults with "saviors" and "messiahs" already at hand, receive a momentary popularity which is anti-intellectual, anti-urban, anti-scientific, anti-technological, even anti-economic. They usually wish to dispense with progress of all sorts, and certainly with all forms of reason. This "second religiosity" is not genuine, has no great future, but is effective for the moment, all the same, as it signals more clearly than anything else the end of the civilization. Spengler thought that we are certainly in such a period now in Western Civilization, though how deeply the decay penetrates it is as yet hard to say. Spengler compared it with the end of the Classical Civilization; when Archimedes, the last of the great Greek scientists, died and the conquering Romans came, almost at the very end. He predicted very deliberately that when this happens to us we will give up the experimental sciences and indeed all exact reasoning.

He was careful to point out how essential the passage of his four stages is in the life of a culture, of which the whole course is self-determined. Cultures pass through their spring-summer-autumn-winter stages in virtue of their own natures; even the end is a natural death in most cases, and not due to external events. Like the life of any organism, its development is in a certain way built into it from the beginning, and nothing external can hinder or accelerate its rate of unfolding. True, certain external factors may kill the culture's organism but they cannot alter its pattern or change its essential traits; it is what it is, and becomes what it must become.

The Special Features of Spengler's Outlook

Spengler's chief aim was to show the decline and coming downfall of Western Civilization. His secondary aim was to show how all civilizations, past and present, disclose the same life-cycle. He did this in a style which shifted continually, from an objective inspection of facts to a calm assertion of universal statements to a subjective and emotional reaction. He was scientist and prophet, historian and literary artist; and it is perhaps these shifts and turns that make his book bewildering and at the same time in its way fascinating, for, buried in mounds of generalizations which are obviously false to fact, there are dazzling fragments of truths and insights.

Most prominent perhaps in all of Spengler's two volumes is his insistence that culture (or civilization) is a highly organized unit, almost like a living biological organism, in which every part is closely related to every other part, each more a part of the whole than what it is in itself.

This is most evident perhaps in the arts, which best and most intimately express the style of a culture. In each culture there is only one style, and that is why it is almost unnecessary for this purpose to distinguish between the various arts. Only the pedants separate music, painting, drama, sculpture, when each is only a mask of the real inner spirit of the culture. Spengler saw the arts as related in a temporal sequence. As the culture goes through its four stages it develops the arts in a definite order, first architecture, then sculpture, after that painting, and finally music. Yet he is able to praise each of the arts in eloquent and even lyrical terms. Music is what frees man from "the tyranny of light," and in chamber music the Western Culture reaches its highest point. I suspect that Spengler, like most Germans, reserved a special place among the arts for music. Even painting, at least in the Western Culture, is dominated by "musical feeling."

One of Spengler's favorite examples in his study of comparative civilizations is mathematics. He thought that every high culture had its own kind, for instance, geometry was an invention of the Classical Culture, algebra of the Magian Culture, and the calculus of the Western Culture. To show this in detail he made a comparison chiefly of mathematics in the Classical Culture with mathematics in the Western Culture. In the Classical world number was regarded as the measure of magnitude, whereas in the Western Culture number was regarded as relation, a distinction no mathematician would recognize, since magnitude certainly is a kind of relation.

There is for Spengler nothing at all beyond the culture-civilization unit. Everything in human life is relevant to it, and there are no eternal truths which reach across civilizations. Everything is contained within them. This means in effect that there is in the broad and extended sense no progress in history, only an endless repetition of forms. Cultures may be the liberating forces, but they are also the restrictive forces, for they contain all forms, all possibilities. Spengler played down the pre-culture phase in human development, all those thousands of years when primitive man first emerged from more anthropoid species, and all those thousands of years when he shared only a primitive culture, similar to that of primitives today.

As a consequence, as we have seen, he does not render very clear an account of the origins of his great culture-civilizations. "Culture," he said, "is not only a grand thing, but wholly unlike any other thing in the organic world. It is the one point at which man lifts himself above the powers of Nature and becomes himself a Creator." A man who possesses systematic knowledge may be educated, but only when he knows history is he born. Cultures, like men, animals and plants, are "inward forms that constantly and everywhere repeat themselves" and this repetition makes the science of history possible.

I don't think anyone else has emphasized as strongly as Spengler how culture-bound everyone and everything is. There is no such thing as universal history independent of particular cultures and civilizations. Each civilization pictures world-history in its own way. Civilizations may be compared, however, and Spengler's whole work is a comparative study of civilizations. He spent a great many pages pointing to the similarities in their life-cycles. As we have noted, each civilization throws up the same set of men and movements in exactly the same stage of its development as does every other.

In addition to this, however (and perhaps in spite of it), Spengler is anxious to have us understand that there are no universal truths, no values, nothing that extends beyond the confines of a particular civilization. We are born, we grow, we decline and die, always within a single civilization which is our own, and we can know no other with the same degree of understanding, experience no other with the same intensity of feeling. How Spengler himself could know this, how he could understand other civilizations to the extent to which he professed to do, he never explained. He must have considered that he was an exception to the rule; there is no other possible explanation.

What Was Spengler's Achievement?

It is time now to take a backward look across the vast drama of human history as Spengler summed it up. Just what did he accomplish and to what extent did he fail? There is something to be said on both sides.

First, then, the accomplishments.

One of the great merits of Spengler's work is the calm and

steady objectivity with which he regarded civilization. The individual and all that concerns him, his thoughts, feelings and actions, are all caught up in the given stage of culture or civilization in which he lives. He may have made the symbols, he may even have made the prime symbols, but they are not arbitrarily his own; they are the representations of forces which prevail in his culture and in which he himself is submerged. He is, so to speak, helpless in the hands of Destiny, which is the direction taken by the stages of culture, and to which even its greatest men are subject. Cultural relativity is the key to the understanding of all human behavior.

He saw that what moves men has more to do with feelings than with reason. When men feel passionately they do something about it. Spengler did not recognize sufficiently that ideas may underlie passions even though a long way off, and so he acknowledged only the influence of the passions. Deep feelings of conviction take the place of calm consideration even though these may be the products of earlier speculations. Cultures or civilizations are very large organisms and live like organisms: compelled by forces rather than by arguments.

Spengler saw the importance of civilizations as units, but so did some of his predecessors, so did Ibn Khaldûn for instance and so did Danilevsky. Spengler's emphasis on the arts was good; too many historians have neglected the arts in their assessments of human culture. He was the first to call attention in the Western Culture of which he was a member to the importance of Eastern cultures, of the cultures of Asia and of the Middle East, which had been neglected except by specialists. His work has considerable artistic value in its own right as a contribution to literature. He wrote with a distinct literary style and relied much on figures of speech. He thought that a metaphor could make certain values plainer and illustrate with emotions the point he was making.

Thus if he had made a bid as a contributor to literature—and perhaps after all his work should be viewed in this way—it could be regarded as a work of art and not as a treatise on history. But then his claim lay mostly in the field of history. To what extent can he be credited with accomplishments in that? In what we have just noted, there is much to remember favorably.

On the debit side, there is something to score against the ultimate value of Spengler's treatise.

First as to his predictions, their validity remains to be seen. Prophets make many predictions, partly on the assumption, I suppose, that people will recall only the ones that took effect, like a man who fires a shotgun knowing that only some of the pellets will find their target. If successful prediction alone is the test of a theory, then Spengler would have proved the worth of his work beyond any question. He has told us in his preface that the title of the book and the chief idea behind it were decided upon as early as 1912, two years before the first world war, when Europe had never looked so prosperous, powerful and invincible. Spengler was able to see what few others saw, namely, that Europe had entered into the stage of its decline.

Surely no outside force can be held responsible for the decline of Europe. In a series of internecine struggles over the control of the rest of the world, Europe has managed to destroy itself. In the wonderful expression of the English poet George Meredith, "We are betrayed by what is false within." This was not evident to Europeans at the time. And yet, in the two masterful volumes which Spengler said he had planned, and named, in 1912, he predicted *The Decline of the West*.

There is a reservation. European culture spread itself afar. North and South America surely continue the traditions, the institutions, the practices, of Western Civilization. The United States at the present time, in the 1970s, does not show any loss of vigor and may in fact have too much. The so-called energy crisis applies only to the fossil fuels, not to the spirit of man. I see no evidence that we have lost any force in any field.

Of course it did look for a short time as though Spengler was right on target. The symptoms were not good. The Caesars did arise as predicted and did battle with the democracies. It took a second world war in fact to get rid of Hitler and Mussolini and to render Franco powerless beyond the borders of his own country. The Western world emerged shaken from that ordeal, but the United States is stronger than ever and showing no signs of weakening. Then, too, there is the rising power of South American nations, particularly Brazil, which can take up the cause of Western Culture if it falters elsewhere. It is faltering in Europe, that is true, but we must remember that the Soviet Union and Communist China are in many ways still echoing Western Culture. Marx and Engels were Germans, and science, which the two giant communist nations seek to develop at home, is the chief among Western discoveries.

Perhaps Western Culture is, as Spengler insisted, in its civilization phase and so doomed, but it is too early to know. Suffice it to say that Spengler was the first to face Europeans and Americans with the fact that what they had was a species of the genus, civilization, and that civilizations do come to an end. Whether that end is soon or in some distant future it doubtless remains true that there will be an end.

Is science a peculiarity of Western Culture? A discovery of the Classical Culture of Greece, it did not reach there the development it has attained in Europe and America in the last three hundred years. Will science be abandoned when Western Civilization disappears? Perhaps; though it is hard to believe that the immense gains in medicine, agriculture and other departments, which have been made by applying the discoveries of the sciences will ever be forgotten altogether.

Will the fact that human beings were transported to the moon and photographed walking there become merely a legend to later peoples and not taken seriously as something actually done in the past? It is possible, of course, yet we cannot be sure and so we cannot credit Spengler yet with proof of the prediction that Western Culture would decline. Stranger things have happened, but none of us will live long enough to find this one out for ourselves.

Spengler announced at the end of his preface to the revised edition of his great work, which was written in 1922, that he was proud to say of it that it was a *German philosophy*. Those last two words he underlined. Well, it was and like other German philosophies it glorified war. In a part of his preface that his English translators left out he had written that he hoped his book "might not be entirely unworthy to take its place beside the military achievements of Germany." This had its limits for him, however; in 1932 he condemned Hitler in no uncertain terms.

Toward the end of the second volume Spengler wrote, "War is the creator of all great things. In war life is elevated by death, often to that point of irresistible force whose mere existence guarantees victory." This was at the end of the first two great wars that effectively brought German power to an end.

The glorification of war was of course not an invention of Spengler's; it was an honored German tradition; Fichte had praised war, and as we have seen, Hegel, one of the most important of the European philosophers, praised it too. It never occurred to Spengler any more than it did to Hegel that a united Germany could lose a war. The love of war had become ingrained in the German temper and it did them in. After the second world war, world leadership passed to the super-powers, while Germany, defeated and divided, no longer amounted to much in a military way. Those who extol the nobility and the virtues of wars generally count on winning them; but Fichte, Hegel and Spengler, to say nothing of Hitler, apparently could not foresee defeat. Had they known, they might have changed their philosophy.

Chapter II
Toynbee's Study of History

Arnold J. Toynbee was born in London in 1889. He was educated at Winchester and then at Balliol College, Oxford, where
he studied the Greek and Latin classics. During the year that he
attended the British Archaeological School in Athens he heard
cafe talk about the foreign policy of Sir Edward Grey. From
1912 until 1915 he taught ancient history at Balliol, then became a civil servant and worked on Turkish affairs in the Political Intelligence Department of the Foreign Office and somewhat later at the Paris Peace Conference. From 1919 to 1924
he was Professor of Modern Greek and Byzantine Studies at
King's College, University of London, during which there was a
year in Greece as a war correspondent for the *Manchester
Guardian*. From 1925 to 1938 he served as Director of Studies
at the Royal Institute of International Affairs, and for the following eight years was again in government service, this time as
Director of the Research Department of the Foreign Office.

It was in June 1934 that the first three volumes of his monumental 10-volume *Study of History* appeared. I came upon
them by accident. In September 1934, my wife and I were

preparing to return from England to the United States. We had only a couple of hours before our departure when I suddenly remembered that I had nothing to read. Boat trips were wonderfully relaxing for me, but books are more important than food. Promising to be back in a half hour, I dashed out of the hotel and off to the retail shop of the Oxford University Press. There I browsed somewhat frantically, finding lots of good things but not exactly what I felt like thinking about at the moment. I had picked up the first three volumes of Toynbee's *Study of History* and I had also put them down. The covers except for the title and the author's name were blank, and at a hasty glance the contents appeared gloomy.

I was just about to depart to meet my deadline when the lone salesman approached me and said in effect, "I saw you pick up the Toynbee volumes. If you buy them and take them along, I will make you a promise. I live on what I earn here and it is not much. But if you do not like them, I will personally buy them back from you."

Not because of that speech but principally because I was in a hurry, I paid the three guineas or so and watched him wrap the set. In the taxi on the way back to my hotel I blamed myself angrily for being an incontinent fool. "Your trouble is," I said to myself, "you have too much money, and so you throw it away on books you don't want and probably won't ever read."

In the rush of getting a family to a train and then onto a boat, complete with all the baggage, I forgot about my extravagance. The next day I picked up the first volume, went out to sit on a deck chair and began to read and did not stop except for meals until I had finished the third volume.

Then I began to look some parts over again, and by the time I arrived home I had accumulated a stack of notes and comments. I was enthusiastic, though with some misgivings, and wrote a critique of the work as it was at that point (there were more volumes to come), but I could not get it accepted in the United States because at that time no one seemed to have heard of Toynbee. Shortly afterward my essay appeared in two issues of the *T'ien Hsia Monthly*, an English language journal published in Peking until the communist takeover brought its existence to an end.

I wrote to Toynbee and an exchange of letters ensued after I pointed out one of the most glaring errors I had found in his books. Toynbee had said that religion is a product of the lower economic classes, the proletariat, while philosophy is a product of the upper classes, the aristocracy. I pointed out to him that Socrates, the philosopher, was the son of a midwife and a stonecutter, and thus a member of the proletariat, while Buddha, the religious prophet, was a native Indian prince and therefore most surely an aristocrat. In the last volume of his monumental work, volume X entitled *Reconsiderations*, he undertook to answer my criticisms but did not reply to these specific points.

We did not meet until 1950 when in the fall we were both invited to participate in a Conference on Uniformities in History held at Princeton University. There one afternoon Toynbee and his wife took me home for tea, and I had a very pleasant time of it. He was most cordial and alert but reserved in both character and manner; a thin and somewhat frail looking fellow whom you would hardly have imagined turning out the immense amount of work that must have been necessary to finish his *Study*. When he plied me with questions about Louisiana, I replied with a long account of the marshes and their polyglot international inhabitants in that intermediate land under water which lay between New Orleans and the Gulf of Mexico, and Toynbee was extremely interested. He was a man of universal learning and curiosity, a pan-provincial who was familiar with the local peculiarities everywhere.

In 1939 the next three volumes were published. That was all before the second world war, and not until after the war did the last four volumes appear. That was in 1954. Between the first six volumes and the last four Toynbee shifted his viewpoint somewhat. I shall indicate the difference later on, but first the reader who has not read them will want to know the outlines of Toynbee's understanding of history.

History is usually studied as an account of the life of nations or of special periods. Toynbee prefers to think of history in terms of societies and more especially of those larger units he calls "civilizations." In the history of the human species civilization is a recent phenomenon. We can find no trace of it more than six thousand years ago. Before that, as we noted in an earlier chapter, there were only what we now tend to call primitive societies, much smaller societies with fewer artificial achievements. Toynbee's study does not attempt to deal with the thousands of years of primitive societies but begins with the species of civilizations and endeavors to show how they fared.

To what extent was Toynbee indebted to his predecessors? I think the answer must be; to a very great extent indeed. He freely acknowledges considerable indebtedness to most of the historians I have dealt with in this book. He talks about St. Augustine, about Vico, about Ibn Khaldûn (he was, I believe, one of the very first Western scholars to call attention to the importance of Ibn Khaldûn, who was at that time almost entirely unknown in the West). He does not mention Danilevsky but does talk about Spengler. Indeed I think that his greatest debt is to Spengler, from whom he learned a lot. This is not to detract, however, from the stature of his achievement, for in his great work he goes far beyond Spengler.

History for Toynbee is an account of the rise and fall of civilizations. There have not after all been so many of these; he lists twenty-one in the entire record of known history, among them the Iranic, the Hellenic, the Syriac, the Indic, the Sinic, the Minoan, the Sumeric, the Hittite, the Babylonic, the Andean, the Mexic, the Yucatec, the Mayan, and the Egyptiac. Considering the long time span it is a short list, and it is therefore interesting that four of these were in Mexico, Central and South America. We would recognize some of them under other names: Persia, Greece, the Middle East, India and China.

There are six such civilizations in existence today: the Western, the Orthodox Christian, the Islamic, the Moslem Civilization, (including the Arabic), the Hindu and the Far Eastern (Korea and Japan as well as China).

All of them, Toynbee thinks, follow the same life cycle; they are born, they grow, they decline and die. The account of these four stages, together with many detailed examples, constitutes the bulk of his contribution to our understanding of history. We may very well, then, give some space to an explanation of just what makes a civilization go through these stages.

The Genesis of Civilizations

The primitive societies that still exist today are largely static affairs, but Toynbee thinks they were not always so. Some civilizations arose from primitive societies which were able successfully to meet new challenges from the physical environment or the human environment, from harsh conditions or warlike neighbors. For instance, when the Sahara and the Arabian Deserts, which had once been grasslands, became useless through prolonged droughts, some of the inhabitants became nomads and moved about in those regions but others took to the marshes and jungles of the Nile Delta where they met the challenge with their new way of life by developing the Egyptian Civilization. A challenge from warlike neighbors came when the natives of Great Britain had to face a Roman invasion.

One of the large differences between a primitive society and a full-blown civilization, according to Toynbee, is that in a primitive society the elders follow the customs of dead ancestors, while in the civilization they follow the creative personalities who gain a following because they are pioneers. Primitive societies on the whole tend to be uniform, while civilizations contain wide differences.

The primitive response in expanding into a civilization accounts for the origins of a few civilizations, but most of them emerge from the wreckage of previous civilizations. All genesis is the result of interaction. Toynbee calls the older civilization the "apparented" and the younger the "affiliated". Greek civilization was loosely affiliated to the disintegrating Minoan Society of the Aegean which flourished before 2000 B.C. The Roman Empire was the apparented civilization, western Christendom the affiliated. The greater part of Toynbee's account is given to this kind of beginning of civilization. The model which perhaps suggested Toynbee's entire system was the "Hellenic" civilization; that is to say, the civilization of Greece and Rome. Greek culture was the smaller and more originative. After a "time of troubles" it gave rise to the "universal state" of the Roman Empire, which collapsed in giving birth to a "universal church" (Christianity), a wandering of barbarian war-bands (the German tribes on the borders of the Empire), and an "heroic age." The Greeks in effect produced the civilization, the Romans spread its benefits throughout the Mediterranean world and beyond.

Before I can describe in detail how Toynbee thinks civilizations come into existence I must explain an important distinction in social classes which he makes for all civilizations. There is always on the one hand a ruling minority and on the other hand a majority. He calls the first the "creative minority" when it is early and productive; it owes its position to one of several advantages: Either its members hold wealth in land or industry in which they find material advantage, or they make a spiritual contribution in terms of the arts or religion.

The majority, which he calls the "proletariat," is for the most part the class of workers. The communists use the word in their way, but Toynbee goes back to its original meaning in ancient Rome, where it meant the class of free men who had no property but who were not slaves. There always are also, Toynbee says, two divisions of the proletariat, an internal proletariat, those who constitute the vast majority of its citizens; and an external proletariat, those who on the outside maintain a pressure on its borders. Civilizations emerge, Toynbee declares, when the dissatisfied internal proletariat of the apparented civilization decides to break away. He gives as an example the early Christians in the aging Roman Empire, who had acquired values, aims and ambitions different from those of the Romans. The Romans were interested in the values of this world and consequently in luxury and possessions, while the Christians, more concerned with their personal salvation in the next world, renounced the pleasures of this one.

Another and more important explanation of how civilizations originate is offered in what Toynbee calls the movement of "challenge-and-response." Toynbee admits one large difficulty: the origins of civilizations are rarely due to a single cause. One such cause surely is the proclamation of a new religious insight and the establishment of a new church which can give rise to a new civilization, as indeed Christianity did. The creative minority of the older civilization has lapsed into the condition of a dominant minority which has ceased to lead and has become oppressive; instead of ruling by charm, by being what everyone else wanted to be, it now rules by force, at the point of a gun. And so the proletariat as a class revolts. The civilization has degenerated from a state of dynamic activity to that of a static condition. The departure of the proletariat has become inevitable and a new civilization has begun.

It is worth noting here that for Toynbee the bridge between an older declining civilization and a rising new one is the institution of religion. The religion is that of the internal proletariat of the older civilization; the religion, in other words, of those revolting against the civilization, not the established religion of its dominant minority. In this way religion functions as a bridge between civilizations, acting as a conductor from the one which is destined to disappear to the new one coming into existence.

The Growth of Civilizations

The second stage in the life cycle of civilizations is the growth stage. The key to it, Toynbee tells us, is contained in the movement of challenge-and-response we noted briefly in the first stage. The growth of civilizations is brought about by those outstanding individuals whose creative abilities enable them to make advances which are to the advantage of the whole civilization.

One of the signs of growth in a civilization is that progress turns from being an external to an internal process. Toynbee's odd name for this process is "etherialization," by which he means the shift of emphasis in growth from a lower to a higher sphere of activity. It was at the height of the Greek culture that it produced the dramatists, the painters and sculptors and architects for which it had been famous ever since. Society after all is a system of relations between individuals, and in the last analysis it depends upon them, usually upon comparatively few of them. With these individuals, each challenge successfully met makes the next challenge necessary, and enables them to prepare for achievement in the coming struggle. The successful meeting of challenges then spreads until the creative advance is characteristic of the whole society. We can see this clearly in the challenge of overpopulation that confronted the early Greeks, especially in Athens. The first response was to employ the military instrument of the phalanx, heavily-armed men with shields touching and long spears overlapping, and the political instrument of the city-state, to create an overseas empire. The early Athenians responded to the challenge also with such a high rate of creativity that the work done in their city became "the education of Hellas," an ideal for all of Greece to emulate.

These two movements: the cultural works of gifted individuals and the conquest of the physical environment are two aspects of the same stage of growth in a civilization. One marks a sort of internal achievement, a definite progress in self-determination through the making of discoveries in the arts and sciences, and the other an external achievement in the extension of control over other peoples. The Greek conquest of the spirit took place in art, literature, architecture and drama. The conquest of matter was the extension of the influence of the city-state of Athens by means of its naval conquest of nearby cities. Footholds were established on the southernmost tip of Italy, in Sicily, and in what is now Libya, at the expense of the native local populations. Together these two achievements comprise a single comprehensive growth.

The motive force in the growth stage of civilization belongs then to what Toynbee calls the "creative minority." This is his name for the leaders of the advances made on the double front of self and society. But they serve also in another capacity which is of great value to the civilization. They serve as models for the society; everyone wants to be like them. They rule not by force but through charm. In this way they are responsible for the unity of the society; it is better integrated because of their efforts. The creative minority is always a small number of people in relation to the total population, but their importance in proportion to their numbers is vastly greater.

The creative minority operates through what Toynbee describes as "withdrawal-and-return," the withdrawal of an individual or of his group for the purpose of making a contribution, and a return for the purpose of sharing the achievement with the remainder of the society. The result is a reciprocal challenge. The minority challenges the majority to accept the terms of the new solutions to their common problems. The majority challenges the minority to convert it to the new way of life. Growth in a society involves a greater differentiation between the parts of the society as well as greater differentiation between societies. Civilizations differ in the character of their achievements; some in the arts, others in the sciences, etc.

The Breakdown of Civilizations

We have noted the two elements which accounted for the growth of civilization: the fact that the creative minority makes advances in the conquest of the spiritual fields of endeavor and in the physical and social environment; and the fact, no less important, that the masses of people eagerly and knowingly take the creative minority as their model and enthusiastically seek to imitate it. Now in the third stage of civilization, which witnesses its breakdown, Toynbee says this imitation loses its spontaneity and becomes mechanical.

One of the first and most obvious effects of the changing relationship is that the society as a whole is without self-determination. It no longer goes in the direction it had chosen but becomes the victim of the forces it has set loose, and goes in whatever direction its actions have determined for it. A society managed in this way has inadequate flexibility, and when troubles accumulate it can only intensify the same kind of efforts it has already been making, chiefly because it cannot continue to present a common front to the world.

The three movements which mark the breakdown of civilizations are: the failure of the minority's creative power, the consequent withdrawal of imitation by the majority, and the resultant loss of social unity in the whole society.

The minority, now no longer creative, is not unaware that the attitude of its followers among the majority has changed, and instead of leading through charm, as it were, the minority now shifts to compulsion and rules by main force. Toynbee calls it the "dominant minority" because it continues to rule, only now at the point of a sword. For the first time a serious split begins to appear in what had been a unified society. The masses become unwilling partners; the society as a whole loses its capacity for self-direction. In the Greek city-states, for example, we see in this period the rise of the tyrants and the beginnings of dictatorship. One of the inevitable consequences is an increase in the power of the military, which often turns its arms against its own people.

Militarism has a price to pay, for the intoxication of victory breeds errors. The arrogance of success engenders rampant ambition and so leads to disaster. When Athens sought to conquer its Greek neighbors, all it accomplished were the wars with Sparta and its own defeat. The disintegration of Greek culture had begun, though all that Athens had sought was a federation of Greek city-states in an attempt to establish defense against the greater power of the Persian Empire.

The Disintegration of Civilizations

In describing the breakdown of civilizations we noted that the division between the dominant minority and the internal prolateriat became serious and caused a split. We must not forget that there is always an *external* proletariat, and when weaknesses show up in the society, the threat of the external proletariat, always a factor, now becomes more imminent. There is a balance in the influence of each of the three actors in the drama of disintegration. It results, curiously, in a new and separate work of creation. The dominant minority gives rise to a "universe state," the internal proletariat to a "universal church," and the external proletariat to barbarian "war-bands."

It should be noted that Toynbee's use of the term "universal" here, though familiar, is erroneous. There has never been a "universal" state or a "universal" church in the sense that the former rules over all living peoples and the latter counts them all as its members. The Roman Empire was said in the first century A.D. to rule over all "the known world," but not much of the world was known. The "universal state" reached out far in every direction from the Mediterranean Sea, more than any power had done before; but there were whole continents still unknown and effectively out of reach.

It could also be argued that there never has been a universal church either. Roman Catholic Christianity numbered a great many people among its adherents, but surely not all, not even all Christians. It is to Toynbee's credit that he pointed out the importance of Greek Orthodox Christianity, which was based on Constantinople and had just as legitimate a claim to be the church founded by the followers of Jesus as had the Roman Catholic Church, a fact which has been largely ignored by most western historians.

For Toynbee, the civilization of Greece gave rise to two "universal states": the Far Eastern Empire and in the west the Roman Empire. (The Roman Empire had grown so large that it had become unwieldy and so had been split into two administrative wings, each with its emperor.) From these two "universal states" there grew the two "universal churches."

The disintegration of civilizations begins, then, with what Toynbee admits is a class struggle. It ends with a creative effort on the part of the three divisions—the dominant minority, the internal proletariat, and the external proletariat—which in time have come to consolidate their positions.

The dominant minority produces the machinery for the operation of a universal state: the laws to preserve order, for instance, and the administrators to govern. To the dominant minority of a universal state Toynbee attributes also the production of philosophy. The philosophers in this sense are always apologists for the conservatives—Toynbee's view of the role of Socrates and Plato.

The internal proletariat, containing as it does many oppressed populations, such as the conquered peoples and the victims of the slave-trade, begins with violent protest but moves on to the gentle production of a "higher" religion. This is how Christianity got its start, and it accounts also for others, Buddhism and Islam, for instance. One of the characteristics of the "higher" religions produced by an internal proletariat is that they owe their attractiveness to alien inspiration—the inspiration of Christianity came to Rome from Palestine in the Middle East—so that civilizations cannot be considered in isolation. Toynbee reminds us of the famous line with which Edward Gibbon summed up his lesson at the end of his celebrated *History of the Decline and Fall of the Roman Empire*: "I have described the triumph of Barbarism and Religion."

The external proletariat, which had been hostile in the past, evoked the response of a military frontier, which stabilized the barbarian war-bands and brought them to rest on the other side. The characteristic products of the barbarian war-bands which constitute the external proletariat, are, surprisingly enough, epic poems. Toynbee is thinking of the epics of Homer, the *Iliad* and the *Odyssey*, which commemorate the "heroic age" of Greece when Greek warriors laid siege to the city of Troy on the Asiatic mainland, but he suggests other examples, such as the celebrated *Song of Roland*, the English *Beowulf* and the Scandinavian Saga.

Most of Toynbee's attention in all four stages of the life-cycle of civilization is given to social movements, but the activities of leading individuals are paramount. We saw for instance what an important part was played in the growth stage by the creativity of a few great figures, in a process Toynbee describes as "etherialization". Now in the disintegration stage we must account finally for the corresponding turn.

When societies begin to disintegrate, Toynbee explains, the characteristics of creative individuals in the growth stage are replaced by substitutes, which occur in passive and active pairs. Instead of creativity there is either complete abandon or rigid self-control: truancy or martyrdom. Instead of the drive which accompanies growth, there is a drift and a sense of sin. On the plane of activity, instead of the attempt to attain to the ideal in the present there is either a search for the ideal in the past (archaism) or for an ideal in the future (futurism).

The course of a universal state is not smooth. It is subject to defeats and rallies, ending in final destruction. Its standardization as an institution enabled it to survive for a long while but in the end could not save it. The universal church may have on the whole a longer history. And the heroic epics may survive as literature.

It is obvious that Toynbee is at his best in describing the disintegration of civilizations, but this is not without a reason. As we have noted, when civilizations decay they leave a deposit of universal states, universal churches and barbarian war-bands, which, being more than products of disintegration, cannot be explained entirely by way of any single civilization. As they are the bridges between civilizations, they require at least two civilizations to explain them. We are now back at the place where we first made our start—the genesis of civilizations. In its last disintegration phase the internal proletariat revolts and, as we saw at the beginning of our examination of Toynbee's account, a new civilization takes its start.

Toynbee's Second Thoughts

The first three volumes of Toynbee's *Study of History* appeared in 1934, the second three in 1939. Then there was world war II in which, as we have seen, Toynbee was busily engaged in working for his government. After the war he returned to his notes, did the final writing and revisions of the last four volumes, first published in 1954, but by that time he had radically altered his viewpoint and shifted his emphasis. The war had had an effect on his thinking, and moreover one of major proportions.

The shift was so great that it amounted to another theory of history. It can be put almost in a sentence. In the first six volumes the universal state together with the universal church and the heroic age of the barbarian war-band had been the *bridges* between a declining and a rising civilization, but in the last four volumes the production of a universal church now becomes the *purpose* for which civilizations exist.

That is so great a switch that Toynbee must almost be charged with being the author of two theories of history, the first an account of how civilizations rise and fall, the second an account of how they produce "world" religions.

The last four volumes are given over to a study of universal states, universal churches and heroic ages. The universal state marks a rally after a time of troubles. It is devoted chiefly to a consolidation of gains. By means of such developments as its capital cities, its standards of weights and measures, its legal systems and its standing armies, periods of peaceful existence are made possible and maintained. But their chief purpose, Toynbee now insists, is to furnish a secure background for a universal church. Modern Western Civilization owes a great debt to the Christian church. However, Toynbee acknowledges that the universal church he is talking about is an ideal and bears little resemblance to the church that exists. The ideal church would surrender to science in every instance where science could establish a legitimate claim, and the ideal church would not make the three false steps that the Christian church has made: usurping the political power of secular authorities, benefitting from an excess of material wealth, and setting up its own institution, its "corporate self," as its idol.

In a final word, Toynbee takes a dim view of the future of Western Civilization. Even if we assume that it can solve the perennial problem of militarism, of economic and industrial regimentation, and ward off the threat of a great famine, there are still the limitations of human nature to be considered.

The Lessons of Toynbee's Theory

There are two sides to Toynbee's work, as indeed there are to everyone's; but in his case the two sides differ widely; we find there great achievements rubbing shoulders with errors so large they sound almost deliberately misleading. Let me get the bad side out of the way first, because, in my opinion, at least, the good outweighs the bad; Toynbee's contribution to human knowledge and culture is a positive and enduring monument.

Perhaps the most general fault to be found with Toynbee's vast *Study of History* is one for which the professional historians have taken him to task. They condemn his work because they have found him wrong on questions of fact. I am afraid it is often true that when the facts do not fit his theory he changes the facts, not the theory—an unforgivable limitation in a historian.

A second fault is his failure to understand science. Science began as the search for the knowledge of natural law and went on to the practical applications of the knowledge gained. The first is called pure science—or, in this country, basic research—and the second applied science. Toynbee identifies science with its practical applications—science for him is applied science and technology—but his limitation is that he never recognized that such a thing as pure science exists. However, pure science is one of the four grand routes—the others are art, religion and philosophy—which men have pursued in their inquiry into the nature of things. In this sense it is closer to religion than to popular mechanics. Without some comprehension of it and of the fundamental changes it has brought about in our thinking, quite apart from its effects upon the development of a scientific-industrial culture, no one can possibly have a thorough grasp of Western Civilization and what it has become since the scientific method was first discovered in the seventeenth century.

That Toynbee knows nothing of this, given his program of analyzing the structure of civilizations, must count as no small shortcoming. It does not affect his analysis of civilizations in the remote past but it certainly does rob his system of its analysis of the present and its predictive value.

In the opinion of many he is guilty of another, and sadder, error. At just that time in history when Hitler was annihilating the Jewish population of Germany and of those other countries the Nazis had conquered, Toynbee chose to disparage the Jews. He has denied this, of course; yet his insistence that the Jews represent an historical holdover, and that, despite their immense contribution to so many cultural fields, they amount to nothing more than "fossils in fastnesses," (an idea adopted from Spengler) can hardly be accepted. This viewpoint has turned many otherwise sympathetic thinkers against him. Modern

Western Civilization is not a "fastness", and the fact is that the Jews have made a positive contribution to it out of all proportion to the smallness of their numbers, which is not exactly how "fossils" behave.

Now for his good side.

On the whole, Toynbee's work deserves more praise than blame, for he has introduced us to a magnificent vista. Indeed the grandeur of his work makes it difficult for the appreciator to render it due justice.

It seems, to me at least, that Toynbee's comprehension of the sweep of history is greater than that of any other historian's. His hypothesis respecting the structure of history is so much more suggestive than those of his predecessors, that he can almost be said to have invented the field of the theory of history even though his contribution to it may not be able to withstand all criticism. Those who have read Toynbee are wiser for it, and this remains true even if they reject his system in the end. For to reject it is to have to substitute another which is more valid and true than his yet covers the same ground.

We certainly owe to him some idea of the importance of Asia in world culture, an idea which has been monstrously neglected in Europe and America generally. The size and duration of Asian cultures: Indian, Chinese, Japanese, to say nothing of those in the ancient Near East, would dwarf what we know about ourselves and our brief tenure in the West despite the immensity of our recent achievements. He has taught us to revive and to value the heritage of Greek Orthodox Christianity for its artistic and scholarly achievements as well as to count it for its historical role, especially since it has been so neglected by Roman Catholicism and by the later Protestant Christian denominations.

Toynbee raises and attempts to resolve many of the leading problems in major fields of human endeavor: religion and politics, science and art, philosophy as well as history. As a result, an adequate discussion of the problems developed in the *Study of History* would require as many volumes as that study itself contains. My primary aim, therefore, is merely to call attention to the immense suggestiveness and importance of his work.

Toynbee may be said to be the first historian who has attempted to make a profound analysis of the form of human history. He brings together many strands of history in an effort to discover the laws of their organization. In so doing he may have taken the first step toward the establishment of the study of civilization as a social science. History as the mere account of change could interest nobody, since there would be nothing upon which interest could take hold; there would be none of the significant similarities and differences by means of which reason operates. Laws represent what does not change and what all historians are seeking is a knowledge of the constants in historical change; Toynbee has taken us a long way toward suggesting what these may be. He tries to analyze cultural structure, and takes the first step toward establishing the field of human social culture as a field of science.

The search for the laws of society, the analysis of the structure of social organizations, and the establishment of the field of civilization as a social science, collectively make certain assumptions. These assumptions rest on a realistic understanding that science is not a study preoccupied with surfaces but must be recognized as the search for independent and objective laws.

Thus if all the laws of social action were to be learned, social life could be controlled in such a way that the errors of the past would not have to be repeated in the future, civilizations would not have to continue to decline inevitably but would find a way to increase the organization of values. And the goal of human endeavor would not be exclusively that of a transcendent other-worldliness but would include the improvement of conditions in the light of a perfection of theory and practice which is always possible and which is called for by "this worldliness."

Whether Toynbee has discovered any of the functions of history in abstract form or not, there is much of value in his work to guide historians as well as to benefit those who count as one of the necessities of an education some acquaintance with the past. His history is a mythological drama, with all the world at all times and in all places as its stage, with a cast of characters made up of all the great individuals who have ever distinguished themselves, and with a chorus of all the masses who have ever surged toward a goal. Toynbee is not afraid to quote Goethe and other mythologists, for he understands that there is a sense in which mythology represents the essential truths of history.

Thus it may be claimed that Toynbee's *Study of History* maintains some truths which rise above the factual errors and oversights which no doubt are scattered throughout the volumes. And what a wonderful scene these truths depict! What a plot the image of civilization unfolds!

If the test of such a work is its inclusiveness of fact and suggestiveness of theory, its picture of the past and its image of a future, then the requirements of permanence are fulfilled to a very great extent indeed. We are broader in vision, richer in understanding, and keener in appreciation because Toynbee has written. For one who has read his work thoroughly it must become impossible ever again to see the world, especially human history, without looking to some extent through his eyes and from the perspective that he has discovered.

Chapter 12
A Comparison of Civilizations

Some Sample Comparisons

We have come a long way in our examination of man's studies of civilizations, ranging through many centuries and observing many approaches. Our review has come finally to an end. We should be able to look back now and try to put some conclusions together. It is only natural that we will want to begin by making comparisons.

The great advantage of the books of men like Vico, Spengler and Toynbee is the wealth of examples to be found in them. The ten volumes of Toynbee take a lot of reading, but it is a fascinating and painless way to get an education.

Like many of my readers, I grew up in an American city and went to public and private schools. I learned the importance of Europe in history and the large part that has been played by the Roman Catholic religion and later by the Protestant Christian Churches. I was not taught anything about the importance in history of the two principal Asian countries, China and India. I imagine that your experience must have been much the same, but these are gaps that can most easily be closed by reading

Toynbee and then by following some of the suggestions to be found in his work.

Studies of civilization may be divided into two groups according as they are optimistic or pessimistic. Some of our authors have been optimists. They have thought that the civilizations of the future will correct the shortcomings of those of the past and present. Theirs might be called utopian theories. Under this classification the work of St. Augustine, Ibn Khaldûn, Hegel and Marx, for instance, may be listed. Those who wrote the truly cyclical theories were highly pessimistic, predicting that man must make his old mistakes over and over again as the cycle swings around to its primitive beginnings. Under this heading we must include Plato, Vico, Spengler and Toynbee.

Both Ibn Khaldûn and Karl Marx saw the intimate connection between philosophy and the state. There was, however, one large difference. Khaldûn thought that philosophy supports the state; Marx held that the state supports philosophy. The foundation of the state for Ibn Khaldûn was a religious revelation, but for Marx it was the product of the domination of a single economic class. Both saw the relationship in terms of some kind of philosophical justification. That Ibn Khaldûn saw, five hundred years before Marx, the importance of the role of philosophy in the life of the state, is remarkable enough.

Perhaps the strongest effect Vico has had in the modern world has been his influence on the Marxists, who have attributed to him the broadly-based thesis that man makes his own history, and have credited him with having discovered not only the class struggle but also its economic causation and its political effects. Such influences are no less genuine because Vico would not have agreed with the way in which his discoveries have been employed; he would not have been a materialist. The greatness of a thinker is perhaps most convincingly displayed when the origins of conflicting intellectual movements can be traced to his work. Vico influenced the novelist, James Joyce, through the conception of the mythological nature of poetry and the eternally-returning cycle; he influenced Marxism through his conception of the class struggle; and he is currently influencing anthropologists through his conception of the theory of the unity of culture.

Some of our thinkers have believed that they were creating a science of society, inventing social science, as it were. This was certainly true of Vico, as it was of Danilevsky; it was even more vigorously claimed for his own work by Marx. Not so Toynbee; he did not have so high an opinion of the physical sciences that he would want to imitate their successes in sociology. The historians with whom Toynbee almost immediately challenges comparison are Vico, Spengler, and to a lesser degree, Marx.

The comparison between Vico and Toynbee is interesting. There are many similarities: both historians, for instance, had a high regard for religion. Vico, although more attracted than Toynbee to the possibilities of science, clung to the conviction that human life could not be meaningful without the preservation of religion, a conviction which Toynbee shared. Vico managed to combine with his love for the church and for science a wholly modern understanding of myths as containing the essential truths of history.

Of course, neither scholar has ever been wholly understood in his viewpoint on myths, and Toynbee must face the combined scorn of a host of historical specialists to whom mythology in any connection whatsoever with history must be condemned. Yet it is probable that his observations in this field will in the end survive such condemnation. For Toynbee's ability to leap from factual details to mythological essentials and back again, with perfect ease and complete logical justification, is a power that even in lesser degree has been possessed by few, if any, historians.

Vico rejected as too one-sided both materialism and spiritualism. He was not willing to confine his investigation to an appeal to God or to a series of unexplained facts. Poetry is individual truth, he thought, but myth is social or cultural truth. A mythology is an attempt to get at essential truths and it was Vico's insight that this mode of presentation of truth is qualitative.

Poetry, then, can be a method of discovery and, as Toynbee

was later to see, this is true of epic poetry in particular; for it is by means of epic poetry, he says, that the defeated barbarians who had attempted to storm the frontiers of a civilization express their frustration. Throughout his *Study of History* Toynbee never mentioned Vico, but in the last volume of *Reconsiderations*, where he replied to his critics, he accepted my comparison of his position on the historical truths with the similar position of Vico on mythologies. It seems clear, from what he says later in the same volume, that his own cyclical theory of history owes much to Vico's and to this extent represents the spread of Vico's influence in our own time.

Although inclined to regard emotional rather than rational achievements as of prime importance, and thus preferring to take religion rather than science as a touchstone for the consideration of civilizations, Toynbee was more analytical than Vico in his historical investigations. Vico did not have available the wealth of historical scholarship, of archeological findings, and of other theories of history, that were at hand for Toynbee. Yet in a comparison of their accomplishments, there are large areas of interest in which Toynbee's analysis is vastly superior. Vico's work contains much of value to the modern world; yet it is probably Toynbee's which will claim, as indeed it deserves, the greatest attention.

Next in the order of thinkers with whom Toynbee challenges comparison is Karl Marx. No systems could be further apart than that of Toynbee, who was concerned with saving Christianity, and that of Marx and Engels, who wanted to develop an atheistic form of socialism. Yet there are similarities. Both Marx and Toynbee attached importance to the tendency of institutions to make a radical change at a certain stage in their development. Marx and Engels call this the tendency of an institution to "turn into its opposite," Toynbee calls it the "reversal of roles." Essentially the conception is the same, although it is put to different purposes.

Another similarity is that of the class-war. Again, although put to different purposes, the ideas are the same. Both Marx and Toynbee regarded power of one class over the others as a symptom of severe social maladjustment. Marx considered it the fundamental malady of the state, one to be cured only by the establishment of a classless society; Toynbee regarded it as symptomatic of social breakdown, correctible only when a new civilization takes the place of the old.

The differences between them are, however, enormous. Marx was almost exclusively preoccupied with the economic aspect of history and deemed it of first importance. Toynbee, not unmindful of this aspect—as witness his excellent discussion of the revolution brought about by the law-maker, Solon, in ancient Athens—did, however, neglect economic aspects in other periods of history. His superiority over Marx as a theorist lies in his recognition of the vast number of other factors which go to make up a full civilization.

In Marx, history is oversimplified. The careful reader is assured that the understanding of events in the past is a comparatively easy matter: it is necessary to remember only that all events at social levels are caused by events at the economic level. Toynbee had no such illusion, and if he failed to solve all the problems of history, he at least awakened us to their complexities, which is as much as any historian could hope to do.

Perhaps the most obvious comparison is that between Toynbee and Spengler. Among contemporaries they stand out as the authors of the most suggestive surveys of human history ever written. We may best understand the differences between them by glancing first at their similarities.

These are indeed many. Both were anxious to construct a theory of history in such a way that all civilizations past and present can be shown to be members of a single species. In both their studies a cyclical theory predominates, and the cycle of the life of civilizations is divided into four stages. Toynbee's quartet of genesis, growth, breakdown, and disintegration is analogous to Spengler's spring, summer, autumn, and winter. Genesis and growth are flourishing periods as are spring and summer; and in both systems the two last periods mark a decline.

Both systems also rest upon a distinction between human beings and physical nature. Spengler, in fact, saw history as "opposed" to nature, while Toynbee made his separation of man from nature rest upon the independence of the human soul from all that happens in this world, a doctrine eventually derivable from Christian theology. Thus both historians are guilty of a mentalist turn. They saw history in terms of what has been thought by men rather than in terms of what men have been led to do by virtue of what has happened to them.

Again, both minimized philosophy and the role of philosophers in social history, and modern philosophers in particular. For Toynbee, philosophers play an unimportant and rather disgraceful role as members of the dominant minority; for Spengler their importance consists in their non-philosophical activities, and he found contemporary philosophers woefully confined to their own profession, and thus lacking in significance. Finally both thinkers took the same pessimistic view of Western civilization; they agreed that the period of creation is over and that only a period of expansion is left.

Great as the similarities are, the differences are more indicative. For where Spengler was mystical, Toynbee was rational; where Spengler appealed to a vague "destiny" to account for change, Toynbee attempted to show the mechanics of change.

Spengler wrote his history during the World War of 1914-18 and he witnessed the defeat of Germany. He attempted to save German leadership by arguing that if Germany was decaying so were all the other West-European nations. Germany's defeat, then, marked for him a leadership in the march backward. If Western nations were going to decline, then Germany would show us her leadership by leading the decline! Spengler's chief interest was in saving German superiority.

Toynbee, on the other hand, at the outset tried to get rid of any notion that England is the hub of the universe, and attempted to judge the development of history impartially. He, too, had something he wished to save; but since that something was "higher religion" in general and what appears to be Protestant Christianity in particular, we may at least note the superior generality of his choice over Spengler's and give him credit accordingly. Thus, marking German decline, Spengler asserted that "there are no eternal truths" to be discovered or known (since Germans could not know them), while Toynbee accepted the existence of eternal truths even if only as the exclusive possession of universal churches.

The last and most important point of contrast between the ideas of the two great thinkers is contained in their description of the rise and fall of civilizations in general. Spengler compared the life-pattern of human society to that of the human organism, a comparison which Toynbee could not accept. Toynbee saw the life of civilizations in the same pattern but attempted to discover and to show *how* civilizations rise and fall. Spengler offered an analogy between significant persons in different cultures merely by asserting that they represent the same movements of society and indicate the same stage in different societies and under different names. He asserted, at a time when the fact was little understood, that all activities in a given civilization are related. Toynbee, however, attempted to show how these relations come about and why they are true. He did not say the ultimate word about the rise and fall of civilizations but what he did say is of immense significance. That he attempted an analysis at all marks his work as of greater importance than Spengler's.

Civilization is a large word and tends to make us think that it is more organized than in fact it is. When it is too thoroughly organized, there is no great progress. A state which tolerates differences is apt to promote greater achievements by its individuals than one which imposes uniformity.

The lines of influence are not always as clear-cut as some of our authors have led us to believe. Until very recently, we were imitating Greek architecture in many of our public buildings;

Western Civilization would be quite impossible without Roman law; the ancient Hebrews gave religion to a large part of the world, if we count Christianity and Islam as the offshoots they surely were; there are markets and restaurants in every European and American city dispensing the food of virtually every foreign nation. No civilization has yet succeeded in spreading throughout the globe, though many have tried. This is all to the good, of course, for there is a richness in diversity that we would all be unlucky to lose. The wealth of a culture may be measured in part at least by the number of influences active in it.

Lessons from the Accounts of Civilizations

Since civilizations are the largest units of man's social organization, the most ambitious of his endeavors, they must somehow contain his secret. They represent in some sense what it means to be human.

The whole enterprise of the study of comparative civilizations has been challenged on the grounds that the student of them is, like everyone else, culture-bound. Any view of comparative civilizations must be crippled, the argument runs, because it is itself taken from a single viewpoint: that is how civilizations look from the perspective of a single civilization but not necessarily how they are. Spengler insisted that every civilization is, so to speak, closed, and can be understood fully only by its own members, a claim which would have cancelled his entire study of comparative civilizations if he had heeded his own warning, for in comparing civilizations he professed to understand them all, at least to the extent necessary to make the comparison.

The criticism is an obvious one, but is it valid?

In the first place, there is no way to tell whether cultures *are* exactly how they look or are *not*. In the absence of evidence one way or another, the question becomes meaningless.

In the second place, the criticism is in the same case as the comparative study. Since both are equally culture-bound, it is difficult to see how the one can be used to destroy the claims of the other. Until a more consistent argument can be made against the comparative study of civilizations, it must be valued for no more than it is worth. It is worth a great deal, I think. All of us are to some extent culture-bound, each of us is locked in a specific civilization; this is so much taken for granted that no one questions its value. We necessarily look at the human species and all its activities from our own narrow perspective. But there are other ways of doing things; some of them may be more valuable and are at least worth inspecting, either to improve what we have or to enhance our evaluation of what we have for different reasons. The study of how others live precludes our ever taking for granted how *we* live.

By way of illustration let us look at some extreme examples of differences in the practices of civilizations, and then by way of contrast discuss the similarities, which are far greater.

The Lessons of Differences

A study of civilizations reveals the virtually unlimited range of courses of action open to the individual, provided it has the approval of custom and tradition. This is true of so many practices that the choice of one example may stand for most others. Diet is as good an illustration of diverse human habits as any. Somewhere and at some time almost everything edible has been eaten and somewhere else everything edible has been prohibited on religious grounds. Ceremonial eating as well as ceremonial fasting is time-honored. That it sometimes seems the destiny of the human species to try everything that can be tried is a sobering thought; we are bound to look twice at the value of practices we hold dear and assume to be superior to all others. The perspective we gain in considering the different social practices of others enables us to see, often with some astonishment, how strange some of our own customs are. In attempting to understand a civilization (including our own) the thing to do is to look for its peculiarities. By way of illustration, I have selected three examples of cultural practices at random (one of them our own): the literary requirements of the Chinese bureaucracy; the slave-rulers of the Ottoman Empire; and the 'destructive creativity' of contemporary American art. Let us take a brief look at each of them in turn.

One of the greatest social institutions of all time was the Imperial Civil Service in China which required competitive public examinations in the literary classics. For all posts in that service, examinations were conducted of the candidate's fitness by his knowledge of the literary classics and his ability to reproduce their style according to the judgment of the best critics of the day. The system, which had been begun as early as the reign of Wu Ti in the second century B.C., bolstered the claims of the Han dynasty, for the Han emperors came from peasants and could not count on a noble heritage. The civil service examinations reached their peak by A.D. 1313 and were continued until 1905.

Three "degrees" were awarded, roughly comparable with our bachelor's, master's and doctor's, and they consisted mainly in the composition of essays and poems on topics selected from the classic literature. The standards by which they were judged were artificial, and style was considered more important than originality.

The Confucian classics, which formed the basis of this education of civil servants, bore little resemblance to the teachings of Confucius or to their influence. But the practice created a new bureaucratic order and made the transition from the older feudal order of aristocrats to the new order of scholars and officials of the centralized empire a peaceful one. Hereditary nobility was no longer sufficient ground for leadership; henceforth it would be a matter of native ability. Needless to add, the new literary practice did not touch the lives of the common people, but it did give a sense of solidarity, an *esprit de corps*, to the members of the civil service.

Secondly, the example from the Ottoman Empire:

The Turkish Janissaries could be called a unique institution.

In the Ottoman Empire the Sultan's troops had the practice of procuring captive Christian slave-boys in raids, and of bringing them up to be soldiers. They were taken young, and at first sequestered in cloister-like palaces and educated in Arabic letters and Turkish arms, both under trained eunuch instructors. After careful examinations and close inspection the best were selected to join the household cavalry. The most promising were educated and allowed to live in some luxury, often rising to be rulers, and even in some cases appointed to the highest posts in the land. They formed the backbone of the Sultan's personal guard, the "new army" or Janissaries (*Yeni Ceris*), who were notable for their devotion to him. The Turks were of course delighted when they found a man of exceptional ability, and gave him responsibilities accordingly. A few were made admirals of the fleet and even advisers to the Sultan. There was no post higher than Vizier Pasha, which Janissaries from time to time held.

Thirdly, the example from contemporary America:

On August 5, 1973, *The New Yorker* Magazine noticed an art exhibit at the Gibson Gallery on West Broadway. The description ran as follows: "The artist engages in such activities as collecting garbage from the studios of his contemporaries and packaging it for display, blowing up motorcycles with dynamite and reassembling the fragments, and stomping on selected debris until it arranges itself to his taste, and this exhibition of the results is accompanied by photographs showing him in the throes of creativity." The artist's name was Arman.

Three cultural practices: bureaucrats as literary critics; slaves as rulers; garbage as art.

The Lessons of Similarities

No one is responsible for civilizations, which lead lives of their own and of which individuals are only the instruments. What an individual does may have effects he did not intend, thus enabling men to build better collectively than they knew individually. In considering this large and somewhat disturbing fact, we ask: How did civilizations manage to become independent? What is responsible for their rise and fall?

If it is true that no matter how much we learn about ourselves we do not control our destiny, then we must look to some other explanation. We will have to study civilizations as such, intensively and with tools specifically designed for the purpose. Awareness endows men with a certain measure of control by resistance. When men are not aware, they must succumb. Knowledge itself may not be power but it makes the application of power possible. Yet the lives of men are directed by just those elements in the culture of which they remain unaware.

Vico was one of the first to understand that in a complex culture there are ideas common to diverse institutions, as when he recognized in the Athenian assembly and court procedures the source of the logic of Socrates. Every culture consists in a comparable set of institutions; the different institutions in a given culture have more in common than the same institutions in different cultures.

Concrete philosophies—those held without awareness by individuals and those imbedded in cultures—have a greater capacity to exercise effects because they function so silently. The essence of a culture consists in the transparent presence of silent ideas which are tremendously influential but at the same time invisible. A civilization, a culture, is a system of philosophy on the move. The core of the operation consists in the transparent operation of invisible influences—a conception not readily grasped. And if the understanding of concrete philosophies is difficult, consider how much more difficult must be the analysis of those larger units called civilizations, of which philosophies are only a part.

No one is wise enough to grasp all the factors that enter into the composition of a civilization. Vico was keen enough to see that anything which remains buried under the social inheritance, however trivial—the coin of common speech, the warnings of superstition, or the recounting of folk poetry—may serve equally as hints of ideas that once had been held, of conditions that had once prevailed. The elements of a civilization are beginning to be known: not only individuals, but also interest groups, institutions, even those different culture traits which refuse to be anchored in any one place.

Civilizations are organizations in which wholes determine their parts—though not absolutely, yet as the expression of a kind of tendency; less tight than organisms; more tight than corporations. We see the picture in the round through the eyes of professional historians, but usually in terms of some common element; in place of the old recitals of kings and battles, we have new accounts, in terms of economics, etc., but with the new approach as with the old, there is always the problem of mistaking the part for the reality of the whole. Other enterprises often commit the same error in terms of a special interest: histories of art, of science, even of philosophy. The special interest can be more correctly understood as the *theory* of the reality of the civilization, not as itself that reality. (I omit religion as a separate item not because I regard it as not important, but because I intend it as inclusive under the heading of philosophy.)

There are no details, however small, that cannot be of help in understanding something of the depth of cultures. Of course some accounts probe more deeply than others, and those I have cited take profound soundings; from them we can learn much.

The philosophy of a civilization grows up within it at the same time that its results occur. Slowly in the society, through the customs, the institutions, the proclaimed preferences, a central core of general ideas is assembled; no one yet knows the mechanism; there are no controls. The rule about "philosophy" in this sense is that it is never known by that name. It seeps into the culture through language, through the arts, the customs, the arrangement of institutions, the contributions of individuals of genius, through other and more subtle means which have not been isolated.

But the philosophy does circulate, and later on, when we are in a position to see the culture as a whole (after it has "ceased to exist" except in history), we may identify it with some degree of reliability. Professional philosophers reflect the features of the civilization; together they show its range. Those periods in which societies are able to formulate their characteristic theories of reality are more influential than others. Thus philosophy may legitimately be regarded as an index to civilization, and the history of philosophy as an index to cultural trends. There is a hidden philosophy in every culture which accounts for its consistency and it is that which the professional philosophers seek to explore.

What Is a Civilization?

What then is a civilization? It is time to be as precise as possible. Civilization may be defined as "the actual selection of some possible pattern of continuing social behavior, considered in its effects upon materials, made according to the demands of a concrete philosophy, and modified by the environment."

An abbreviated version of the definition is available and may in fact be more illustrative. "Civilization is the social use of materials." This suggests of course the alteration of materials by men to make artifacts for their specific needs and, later, the alteration of the men by the artifacts. In a word, ideas precede them and there is a feedback from them. If that makes my second definition too simplistic, I suggest that we settle for a third. "Civilization is the works of man and their effects (including their effects on man himself)."

I have been employing the word "artifacts" to stand for the works of man, but it must be remembered that two kinds of artifacts are made and used: tools and languages. A language contains in effect the history of a civilization. Artifacts once constructed are preserved, copied, modified. The result in any living society is an accumulation of the works of the dead: of books, buildings and machines; of customs, formulations and abstractions. We live out our lives in an artificial world largely provided for us by those who went before. We live in the environment provided for us, as a matter of fact, by five thousand years of civilization. Societies live on and by their inheritance, modified by whatever adjustments are required by changing conditions. There is a total establishment which is carried along as best it can be in the face of new challenges.

Thus philosophies, too, are artifacts: they exist in cultures as systems of general propositions which underlie the broad consistency of the culture, and they are reflected in the writings and oral teachings of the professional philosophers. In other words, there are such things as naturally-occurring philosophies, and the range of these is demonstrated by the disagreements of the philosophers. Given an ongoing civilization, then, it ought to be possible to describe it as a set of ideas-in-action thrown up by the course of events.

The extreme range of a civilization is seldom known to those in it, and almost never experienced as such by them. How many persons in a modern western scientific-industrial complex have visited a slaughterhouse or the children's ward of a large city hospital? How many have known the life of a forest ranger, of a pure mathematician? How many have lived as a housemaid at one time and an industrial executive at another? Failing the special insights available only from such complexity of experience how could they ever agree as to the character of the civilization? How could they know that all of us, whatever our station in life, have something important in common?

The structure of a civilization is so strong that when we count the individual, together with the artificial environment he has fashioned for himself and with which he now interacts, it becomes clear that he is much like a wave in the ocean of humanity. He is typical because there are so many like him. It is difficult not to accept the reality of a class when it has so many members. We are all part of some larger destiny that is working itself out in ways that none of us understands but that the best of us assist in bringing about in that broadest of organizations we call civilizations.

The recent gains in the knowledge of what is called pre-history, the history of the ancestors of man, and the history of man before settled civilizations and written records, have done much to alter the notion that there is no progress. For in the construction of artifacts progress has been considerable, but for humans —where it counts, namely, in the character of his motives— there has been no gain.

The point is important enough to bear re-emphasis: *there has been no progress in motivation.* Like prehistoric man, we still want to help some of our fellows and hurt others, we try to be kind to friends and fierce to enemies, as Plato suggested; only, we have found some fancy ways of doing both: we have hospitals instead of magicians, nuclear missiles instead of bows and arrows. The artifacts have been improved and made more efficient as the size of the populations that had to be assisted or killed increases; but the paradox of motivation has remained constant.

The opposite aims of human nature are nowhere to be seen more on the surface than in the conduct of religions. The peaceful intentions of a founder are often followed but not by as many as practice intolerance and persecution in his name. How many religions can claim no militant movements? Is not militarism the defeat of the ideals of a founder in almost every case? Men pursue peace and war.

It is certain that the human population, looked at from the longest view of history, tends to increase rapidly. People must therefore learn more about how to live together. But there are great advantages in variety, in having different civilizations all existing in the world at the same time. The richness of difference cannot be denied—in painting, in forms of dance, in language, in life.

We noted in the first chapter the benefits to the individual from the experience of cultures other than his own. Travel is of course a way of seeking enrichment of this sort. If our globe were spanned by but a single civilization there would be no advantage in it. What we want is the variety of civilizations without the conflicts they have produced. Only tolerance of differences can enable us to see the ennobling advantages of variety in humanity.

Chapter 13

The Shape of History

How Do Civilizations Get Started?

What lessons can we learn from the foregoing accounts of civilizations? What is a civilization really like? The answers to these questions will tell us something about the shape of history.

It has often been pointed out that, while civilizations are not living organisms, they do have a life-cycle resembling that of organisms. We know that they come into existence, grow, flourish, decline and die. We have now to ask how and why they do so.

There really are two questions here: how did the first civilizations arise, and how do later civilizations emerge from earlier ones? I have tried to answer the first question in chapter 2. Here we shall deal with the second: how do later civilizations get started? Of course no one knows with certainty. We can only conjecture.

The most pressing of all human needs is security. What absorbs the interest of every individual is the immediate problem of survival; how to continue his existence. And there is a further need, which is to obtain ultimate survival, the continuance of existence after death. This is everyone's secondary interest. Both the need for immediate and for ultimate survival evoke different methods, depending upon the inheritance and the environment in which people find themselves.

In the debris of a dying civilization, the human societies with their beliefs, their tools and their institutions, lie all the materials which will be reshaped and so furnish all that is needed for the emergence of a new civilization.

All that is required in addition is a new discovery or a new insight. Sometimes this has taken the form of a new technology, sometimes the form of a new religious claim. The new religious claim made in the name of Jesus was responsible for the rise of Christian Civilization in the Middle Ages.

In the seventeenth century the scientific method of discovery was a new technology and gave rise to European Civilization. Christianity promised an immortal spiritual life to the faithful. The applications of science offered a more abundant material life to its practitioners.

Interest in survival has taken many forms and led to many avenues of investigation. In some civilizations it has taken the form of artistic endeavor. This was true of Stone Age man and of the civilizations of Central America, of the Mayans and the Aztecs, for instance. In Greece the search by means of philosophy was added to that of art. In Asia, particularly in India, the ancient civilizations did not look outward but inward, and sought some sort of security in the cultivation of the self. Art, religion, science, philosophy, all began as questions and ended with material constructions intended to find answers to the questions. Of course they did not; but *it has been in the frozen answers to unanswerable questions that civilizations have consisted.* We are all beneficiaries of the men of genius who were responsible for the artificial environments in which we live.

We can see now that civilizations get started as a result of new beliefs, beliefs in new ways of obtaining immediate or ultimate survival.

Beliefs in the supreme importance of life after death governed the ancient Egyptian and the medieval Christian Civilizations. As the life after death was understood by the Egyptians quite differently from the way it was understood by the Christians, their civilizations were different.

Perhaps the most dramatic contrast is to be found in the Pre-Columbian civilizations of Central and South America. With a technology that was no more advanced than the Stone Age they managed to combine achievements in the arts that would rival the most advanced civilizations. The beliefs which led to such diverse activities obviously were not questioned. They underlay all others and led to particular forms of behavior in every walk of life.

People are what C. H. Waddington has called "authority-acceptors." They tend naturally to embrace some sort of fundamental belief; indeed they seem to need one. The younger they are the easier it is to hold a belief; the more absolute the belief the more readily it is grasped. This is the reason why Mohammed met with such immense success among the desert people of Arabia and why Buddha had such a tremendous impact on India.

To sum up: a civilization is the accumulation of the thoughts, feelings and actions of a people considered in their total effect upon the environment and in the consequent reactions of the altered environment back upon them. It takes a long time for the psychology of individuals to have an effect upon the materials in their environment—that is what civilization comes to. Given a people who have recognized a common cause, its thoughts give rise to the ideas which constitute its beliefs, its feelings are responsible for its choices of aims and for what it does in the arts, and its actions lead to the material side of its efforts toward cooperation and aggression. The conflicting motives which are to be found in every individual, his will to constructive and destructive actions, in the end find expression in the life of civilizations, the first for their growth, the second for their decline.

We are now ready to take a closer look at a few examples of

civilizations. Since the two crucial periods are rise and decline our best examples come from those periods, and are selected from those which are best known, that is to say, those of which the details have been observed and recorded and the features stand out most clearly. For these reasons I have chosen the origins of the Muslim Civilization and the decline of the Greco-Roman Civilization as well as the life-cycle of European Civilization.

The Origins of Muslim Civilization

How is a civilization started? The question is difficult enough to answer even in a more modest version: how is a country started?—which has in fact been asked. Once the British had retreated from American shores the Founding Fathers had to face this question. The Russians faced it after the Revolution of 1919, when attempts were made to sweep away the influences of the Czarist regime and begin anew. More recently, after the Israelis had carved out a small territory for themselves, the authorities there approached friends seeking information about starting a country. They were in need of a constitution, a flag, customs, money, postage stamps—all the paraphernalia that every country has and that all take for granted.

One of the many ways in which civilization often begins is with a religious inspiration. Toward the end of the fifth century A.D., probably in 570, an Arab was born in Mecca whose leadership and teachings were to form the basis for a new civilization. Before Mohammed the Arabs were living in scattered tribes, tending flocks and engaging in petty skirmishes. The desert Arabs in Mohammed's day, as our own, were primitive. They had few artifacts, no society beyond the tribe, managed to exist in an environment of sand and occasional palm trees, and clothed, fed and watered by camels.

Religion was a local affair; there were probably as many trib-

al gods as there were tribes. There must have been some sem-
blance of unity, however, for Mecca was considered a sacred
spot by all, and by common agreement the fighting was halted
for four months each year so that visits could be made to a temple full of idols, the *Kaaba*, which also contained a particular
black stone, about the size of a man's hand, considered especially
holy.

Mohammed made his living as a camel-driver moving with
the caravans, those trains of the desert. He was lucky to find
work in one owned by a wealthy widow named Kadijah, for she
fell in love with him and married him. He was twenty-five at
the time, and she was forty. As he traveled back and forth across
the desert with his merchandise-laden camels, his thoughts
turned to religion, and he soon became convinced that God was
sending him messages which it was his duty to relate to mankind. In his travels he met many Christians and Jews, and no
doubt in this way made the acquaintance of the Old and New
Testaments. He was only semi-literate and probably had to
have the books read to him. From them he learned many ideas
which he later used.

When he tried to convince people that the angel Gabriel had
appeared to him in his dreams and conveyed the outlines of a
new religion, he was met with ridicule. In fact his enemies
sought to kill him, and in 622 he fled to Medina, a friendly
neighboring town, a flight which the Arabs still call the *Hejira*.
For the next eight years there was desultory fighting between the
inhabitants of Mecca and those of Medina, until finally Mohammed felt that his following was large enough, marched on
Mecca and conquered it. Within ten years of the *Hejira* Mohammed had won the support of all the Arab chiefs, and his
new religion, which he called *Islam*, meaning "submission to
God," had replaced all others throughout the Arabian Peninsu-
la.

At the center of the Muslim religion is the *Koran* which pur-
ports to contain the sayings of Mohammed as his followers

wrote them down, very much in the same way that Jesus was reported in the Gospels. Mohammed believed himself to be the last and greatest in a long line of prophets, after Abraham, Moses and Jesus, and the one who had brought the last and greatest of religions to mankind. Like the Jews he prohibited the worship of idols (except the black stone) and forbade the making of graven images.

The basis of Islam is the belief in a single God by a prosletyzing people. The Jews, the Muslims insist, do not seek converts, and the Christians worship more than one god.

A good Muslim may have four wives and as many concubines as he can afford, but he must abstain from alcohol. Besides the usual virtues, such as seeking justice and avoiding pride, there are five commands which he must obey. First, he must recite the short creed every day, "There is no god but God, and Mohammed is his prophet." Prophet, not saint or god; that is why his followers prefer to be called Muslims rather than Mohammedans. Secondly, he must pray five times a day: just before sunrise, just after noon, before and after sunset, and at the end of the day. Thirdly, he must fast during the whole month of *ramadan* from sunrise to sunset because that is the time when God sent Gabriel to him with the *Koran*. Fourthly, he must give alms to the poor. Fifthly, he must make at least one pilgrimage to Mecca during his lifetime.

The *Koran* promises a day when the heavens shall be opened and the mountains reduced to flying dust; all men will receive their judgment; the wicked will be punished, they will be banished to hell to burn in torment forever, but if they have been faithful to the precepts of the *Koran* or better still if they have died fighting for Islam, killing all those Christians and Jews who resist conversion, then they will live in luxury forever in Paradise, where wine can now be drunk and where there will be an endless supply of "sloe-eyed maidens with swelling breasts."

There was no separation of church and state. Mohammed's successors had the title of *caliph*, or representative, and ruled with absolute power in both spheres. Two generations after Mohammed's death the Arabs conquered Syria, Egypt and Persia; they held all of Arabia, of course, and added North Africa to it, then Spain. They were not turned back in southern Europe, in fact, until they were defeated at Tours in 732. They retreated from what is now France, never to return, but remained in Spain and established a Moorish kingdom there. Turkey was also made into a Muslim country, but Constantinople, the Byzantine Christian capital, held out until 1453.

By 750, no more than 180 years after Mohammed was born his followers had established their conquests in Asia Minor North Africa and Spain; the Ottoman Empire was the largest, and at the time the most enlightened, of ancient regimes. What the Muslims had founded was of course a civilization. The arts of peace were pursued vigorously. Muslim architecture, for instance, achieved many triumphs, of which examples, from the Taj-Mahal in India to the Alhambra in Spain, may be seen to this day. And it was Muslim Civilization which preserved Greek science until it could be handed on to the Europeans.

The followers of Mohammed probably number more today than they ever did, but their civilization has atrophied and is entirely at the mercy of those stronger nations which have embraced pure science, applied science and technology. Today dirt, disease, ignorance and illiteracy are the lot of masses throughout the Moslem world, though the newly-found wealth from oil promises better things.

The whole of Muslim Civilization may be said to have been founded on the notion that Mohammed was a "true" prophet. What, it may be asked, is the difference between a true prophet and a false one? The true prophet succeeds in gaining and holding a following, the false prophet does not. In that case Mohammed was a true prophet: Islam can today count on 300 million people. But there is more to it than that. The following of the true prophet persists and even spreads widely after his death.

Yet the matter is not quite that simple: why does one succeed where many fail? What is there about the one who succeeds which sets him apart? Surely not his personality; who knew a hundred years later what Mohammed was really like? It must be something in his message rather than his person that had universal appeal.

Here perhaps is the secret of the origin of cultures, and it is, according to the well-turned phrase, a mystery wrapped in an enigma. Whatever it is, it serves as a focal point toward which many thoughts, feelings and activities are drawn. As a movement of this sort gains momentum it pulls into its orbit and retains customs and traditions which had been inherited but which had lacked organization. Religion leads to culture, and culture to civilization, as the radius of influence widens.

The Decline of the Greco-Roman Civilization

We have looked at the rise of one civilization; let us look at the decline of another.

The rise and growth of the Roman Empire were probably due to the insight that the achievements of the Greek city-states, in particular Athens, could be made international. The Romans did not invent Greek culture but extended its benefits throughout the Mediterranean world. What the Romans had may have been of a secondary kind, but it was what was needed: a talent for social organization and communication; good government and good roads.

It would be fair to say that the Roman Empire at its height corresponds to the reign of Octavian from 30 B.C. to A.D. 14, which was the beginning of two centuries of peace and prosperity. When Octavian (Augustus) died at the age of 75, after 44 years of successful rule, his descendants were able to carry on for another half century with the impetus he had given to the Empire. What then was responsible for its decline?

When we look at it carefully we see a succession of small disasters and small failures, none of them anything significant in itself but all adding to a down turn which, had the force for organization been greater, would not have counted so strongly—among them, bad rulers like Caligula (37-41), and Nero (54-68), the fire of 64 in Rome, the struggle of military commanders for the throne, the decrease of farming in Italy, plagues, trouble with the finances of the Empire, increased taxation, cheapening of the coinage, transformation of the frontier army into a kind of militia, finally military revolts and successful barbarian raids.

The decline was intermittent; before the two centuries of peace there had been one century of revolution (133-30 B.C.); and after the two centuries of peace from 30 B.C. to A.D. 170, there was a second century of revolution, A.D. 180 to 284. Then there came fatal attacks from two quarters: barbaric invasions from the north and the revival of local power in the east, particularly in the Persian provinces. The fall of Rome to the army of the Visigoths, led by their king Alaric in the summer of A.D. 410, shook the entire world. Finally, a new religion, Christianity, which looked like Mithraism, the religion of the Roman legions, appeared and helped to tear apart the fabric of the established Roman social structure.

Like the puzzle of the rise of Islam, the reason for the Roman decline eludes us, until we remember the theory with which we started this chapter, namely, that a civilization begins when a new and absorbing interest, usually ideas calling for vigorous action, takes hold and stimulates a people into becoming a dynamic force. It would begin to decline presumably when the actions generated by those ideas had all been exhausted.

Perhaps a loosening of organization is the result of a falling away of interest in the aims which held it together. No matter what the answer, it only puts the question back a little: why the falling away of interest? If all that could be done to achieve the aims was done, a decline was inevitable. There is no plateau in human affairs; they grow or begin to perish. When the Romans had achieved all that they could, the resultant prosperity was a sign that affairs would not remain so for much longer.

It is time to look now not at how one civilization arose and another declined but at the life-cycle of a whole civilization, though we can do so here only in a brief and sketchy way.

The Life-Cycle of European Civilization

Our example of such a life-cycle of civilization is the European —the Western—Civilization.

When the defeated Christian crusaders returned from the Holy Land, carrying with them the Greek classics which the Arabs had translated but which had been unknown in Europe throughout the Middle Ages, and when the Christian monks began to show an interest in scientific theory and experiment, it marked a turn from dedication to life in the next world to a burning interest in life in this one. The artists began to study anatomy and the scientists the world of nature which had been their little-known environment. Little did they recognize that they had started Europe along a path that would end in the establishment of democracy, in the paintings and sculpture of Italy, the theatre of Shakespeare's England, the music of Germany. The day when a people acts on its new interests is the day when a civilization is born.

At the end of the Middle Ages in Europe there suddenly appeared a number of new concerns. These have been grouped by historians under the name of the Renaissance, the rebirth; it was a rebirth of Greek and Roman art, literature and learning, but it was much more than that. As the power of the Roman Catholic Church declined, other attitudes and activities came to take its place. Instead of looking to the next world in terms of general principles such as Church dogma, there was an absorbing interest in the things of this world; it was as though men were seeing them for the first time.

Led by the new humanists who wanted to examine what the natural man was like and sought only what was good for him, there were other developments. In the Middle Ages men had had three main interests: God, man and the relations between them. But now for the first time it seemed that the relations between them were mediated by nature; since man was an animal imbedded in nature and nature was the creation of God, it behooved men to examine how God's creation worked, and so they set about examining man and nature. For the first time, perhaps, sense experience replaced revelation as the instrument for searching out truth. Travels and voyages of discovery aided this newly found importance of what the senses disclosed, and so men set sail for the Indies and found the Americas, an event which was to widen horizons more.

Along with sense experience and the natural man went a belief in his individualism. The human being became more important than the state, for example, although nationalism grew up in this period also.

Science, with its observations by means of sense experience, its experiments with specially designed instruments, and its mathematical calculations from the results of experiments, was perhaps the supreme achievement of the Renaissance. The Greeks had discovered the scientific method but had not learned to build on each other's work which would have enabled a new scientist to start not from the beginning of an investigation but from where the last investigator had left off.

The thoughts and practices that characterize the Renaissance had one idea in common: the supreme importance of the individual. History moves in terms of the acceptance of ideas and of their broad application in practice, and individualism was a new idea.

Nature, and man, who was as much a part of nature as any other animal, that was the fresh interest, and an exciting one. The importance of sense experience was what got the new civilization going. The spread of that interest also saw its growth.

Soon Europe was humming with newly-found activities: the Renaissance artists and scientists, the explorers and, spanning a few centuries, the new government of democracy and the new European nations to put it into practice, all amounting to a new civilization in its growth phase. The Renaissance occured over a span of years beginning in the fourteenth century and lasting through the sixteenth. In the next two hundred years Europe and its colonies consolidated their position. The hold of the Roman Catholic Church was broken and the new Protestan⁻ sects, which swept away the old dogma and sought a return to the origins of Christianity, established their right to be practiced, though only after a series of wars as bloody as any have been. The establishment of colonies, some independent of the home countries in Europe, some not, but all pursuing some form of European Civilization, moved swiftly to become the reality in the "new world."

The spread of European Civilization is still in progress. Communism and science as established in Russia and China are both European inventions, though communism has not been practiced in western Europe.

Some would make a different interpretation: that the Soviet Union and Communist China represent a new Asian Civilization and not an extension of the European. Mine is that European Civilization has had two wings: the American and the Asian, just as ancient Greece gave rise to the two wings of the Roman Empire, the Eastern based on Constantinople and the Western based on Rome, as evidenced by the passing of military and political power from the three European countries—England, France and Germany, where it had lodged for so long—to the three new super-giants, the United States, Russia and China.

In an impartial view of man today, we see a bundle of paradoxes: a man who has accustomed himself for generations to city life, in which almost everything natural has been altered through human efforts; who has also brought with him through the millions of years of his descent a forest creature more at home with the life of the hunter—Jacquetta Hawkes has observed that hunting is still his preference, to which he returns when he can—who was a cannibal longer than he was anything else and who has now given up cannibalism. He no longer eats the bodies of his enemies but he still kills them; and as there are more of him and more of them, wars now have to be occasions for wholesale slaughter, which of course is what they are. We see man, then, caught between the co-operation which is required of him in the Age of Science and the aggression which was required of him in the Stone Age in which he lived for hundreds of thousands of years.

Civilizations are collective efforts on the part of man to give up his aggression in favor of co-operation, but what has actually happened is that both have been surrendered to the state, which imposes co-operation upon its citizens and practices aggression against their enemies, the citizens of other states.

Long peaceful periods in history have never existed. However much we may like to think that all men prefer them, or even that most men do, it is not borne out by the facts. We shall not have attained to the full condition known as civilization until we learn to achieve a full life for the individual without endangering the lives of individuals in other civilizations. Thus civilization is an aim rather than an existing state of affairs. The hunter in man will have to be banished before he can learn to live at peace with the entire human species. The only way in which he can hope to avoid wars is to find some satisfactory basis for emotional security other than absolute belief.

Can we expect European Civilization to survive indefinitely? No other civilization has: each has had its time of flourishing and then has departed. There is no reason to suppose that European Civilization despite its extraordinary success will be an exception. There are enough difficulties confronting us now to make the belief in a period of decline acceptable. The weapons of war are so lethal that they make even the survival of the species doubtful. The machinery already exists for the establishment of a global society which could through intensive co-operation save us from such a fate.

It is in any case, a race between aggression and co-operation, both greatly extended in scope. I would be inclined to bet on the aggression. Fighting is too old in the human animal and too native to man for anyone to expect that he will give it up. The current posture of the most powerful nations with their nuclear weapons, imitated by the smaller nations, leaves little room even for the hope that things are never as bad as they look and so never turn out as expected. There are too many variables in individual and social life for anyone to be able to take them all into account.

The Underlying Structure of History

We are all familiar with the theme-and-variations form of musical composition in which the composer first announces a melody, and then works out variations, all of which bear resemblance to the theme. One of the clearest as well as one of the most beautiful examples of this kind of composition is "Brahms' Variations on a Theme by Haydn".

The bare bones of the development of a civilization looks very much like this form of music.

In the example of European Civilization I gave in the previous section, the adoption of that set of ideas which is consistent with the supreme importance of the material individual, and hence not only of human individuals but also of everything to be found in nature, corresponds to the announcement of the theme. Everything that followed consisted in one set of variations or another, all on the same theme.

I cannot emphasize strongly enough that by "set of ideas" I do not mean anything superficial, as when one says casually, "I have an idea . . ." I refer to the kind of profound ideas that are contained in the most fundamental of all beliefs, the beliefs about reality which lie at such a deep level of our being that we are often unaware that we hold them. These are the ideas that move men, the kind which lead to crucial and often fatal actions.

When there are no more variations on the original theme, the civilization loses impetus, and so ceases to make any progress. In that stereotyped condition in which it goes on repeating itself, it may last for centuries, even millenia, provided no external force disturbs its delicate balance.

Of course toward its weakened end it may fall prey to some social force that threatens its existence or challenges its power. Civilizations may decay from within or receive a mortal blow from without.

A brief comparison between the crucial events in the life of the individual and those in the life of a civilization may be helpful though it could easily be carried too far.

The most important moment in the life of an individual, his birth, is the one over which he can exercise no control. Over many subsequent events he can have some control, at least to some extent; the choice of a mate, the choice of a career, the decision to take advantage of the opportunities that chance presents to him.

Civilizations operate in much the same way. That they do lead "lives" of their own is demonstrated by the fact that they never go exactly in the direction their leaders have chosen for them. There are too many variables, too many unknowns, for any individual or group to grasp or direct. A true leader is one who senses which way the wind is drifting and gets there ahead of the procession. You may conjecture that a series of events will have to happen (though you may not know them in detail) if you can first determine what happened before and what that must lead to. History is a mixture of necessity and chance.

It is not easy for an individual to see how much of his thoughts, feelings and activities are decided for him by the civilization in which he grows up. Many of our beliefs are acquired in the course of daily affairs without our awareness. The same is true of our customs. When an inhabitant of Calcutta wishes to sit down he thinks nothing of squatting on his heels, a New Yorker finds that position impossible. Shark fin soup may be a rare delicacy to the Chinese; Americans avoid it. We are immersed in, bound by, our civilization, hardly recognizing to what extent that is the case. It is everyone's conviction that things have always been pretty much as they are now, allowing only perhaps for very minor variations. Nothing could be further from the truth. We are living at this moment somewhere along the life-line of a civilization, in which certain beliefs and practices are routine and native, a civilization, however, which will some day decline and die, to be replaced by another in which all that we stood for and much that we accomplished will seem strange and outmoded, at best quaint.

History, broken up into the units we have called civilizations, is not an even and uniformly-flowing affair. Nothing in the universe remains the same forever. Civilizations, like plants and animals, like planets and suns, come into existence, endure for a while, and then perish, to be replaced by others like them and yet very different. If we look carefully, we can see though it be from a great distance and over a long prospect of time, that history has a rhythm that is determined by the comings and goings of those organizations of men and artifacts that we have come to call civilizations. We do not know why this procession moves as it does, but we are beginning to learn something of *how* it does. Perhaps in the remote future we will also learn *why*.

Chapter 14

The Prospect of
Civilizations in Space

Life Elsewhere in Space

As I write, it is well known that the United States and the Soviet Union possess enormous nuclear capability in weapons. In a war they could put an end to all civilization and perhaps even bomb each other back into the Stone Age. It is therefore no science fiction that the hope of human survival may lie elsewhere, either on some other planet in the solar system or farther out in space.

In chapter 2 we began our account of civilizations by looking at the immense sweep of time that had been required for man to evolve on the earth and for him to develop civilizations. We might end our survey by looking at the prospect of civilizations elsewhere in space. Most is guesswork.

Hitherto our knowledge of civilizations has been confined to the surface of the earth, but that is likely to change. There are other planets in the solar system and millions of solar systems in this and other galaxies. In the vastness of the universe there are so many millions of stars like our sun that the prospect of millions of planets like the earth is a likely one, with other life, even civilizations like and unlike our own. The knowledge will come slowly but it will come. After all, space research is very young; the first earth satellite was not launched until 1957. The first man to land on the moon did so on July 20, 1969.

The earth is apparently the only planet in the solar system with an atmosphere that man can breathe, hence it is probably the only man-inhabited planet in that system. The requirements for life are many: air of the right sort, temperature, gravity, an abundance of water, other conditions in more or less degree. Yet according to the astronomers our situation is far from unique. It has been estimated that civilizations are forming in our galaxy alone at the rate of one every ten years. If there were only one civilization for every hundred thousand stars there would be millions of civilizations.

With so great a profusion of opportunities there must be life on some of these planets quite different from our own. All life on the earth is based on carbon, which has a high combining-power. But perhaps elsewhere in the universe there may be life based on silicon, which has the same high combining-power. What silicon creatures would be like we lack the power even to imagine. An enormous stretch of the imagination is also required when we consider the use of ammonia in place of oxygen as a solvent. It is present for example in the atmosphere of Saturn.

Another exciting prospect is that life elsewhere may be like ours but older. If biological evolution works everywhere, as natural laws seem to, on other planets remote from us there may be creatures as much advanced over us as we are over ape and chimpanzee. Certainly there must be civilizations less advanced than ours, in a shorter period of evolution, and others evolved beyond us, over a longer time, and I can think of nothing more exciting for mankind than to make contact with them and to learn in this way what is in store for the human species in the distant future.

The search for extraterrestrial life has been established as a

continuing form of investigation. If there are civilizations elsewhere in the universe, what is the best method of communi-
cating with them?

In many astronomical observatories, chiefly in the United
States and the Soviet Union, time on the big radio telescopes is
being programmed to listen to signals from outer space, for it is
believed that perhaps there are beings in distant civilizations
who may be trying to get in touch with us. The astronomers
who are directing this program are not visionaries, neither are
they writers of science fiction. They are hard-headed investiga-
tors who will accept nothing less than undeniable fact to support
their beliefs. Yet they are so sure from the evidence that life
exists elsewhere that they are willing to spend part of their
precious time looking for signs of it. Of course merely the increase in the number of radio telescopes oriented to record in-
coming signals sharply increases the probability of discovering
other civilizations merely by chance.

A word of caution in the midst of this intriguing prospect
might be in order. All signs received from outer space must be
assumed not to be human until proved otherwise. The final
warning comes from one astronomer. He has pointed out that
science relies in the last resort only on tests by observation and
experiment. Thus far neither test has occurred in connection
with civilizations situated elsewhere in the universe even though
the evidence is strong that they do exist.

Astronomers have not been content with a passive role as list-
eners. They have sent probes into outer space. On March 3,
1972 a spacecraft named *Pioneer 10* was launched from Cape
Kennedy, intended to explore Jupiter, and then, accelerated by
Jupiter's gravity, it was supposed to leave the solar system, the
first man-made object to do so. Considering that it may encounter other civilizations or similar probes sent out by them, a
plaque was attached to it containing a message, including a picture of a man and a woman, so that whoever encountered the
spacecraft would have some idea of what the creatures who sent

it looked like. Whether anything comes of the effort or not we will never know, only some future generation may, yet it is an intriguing idea just the same and was well worth undertaking.

It is now possible to send an unmanned but not a manned spacecraft outside the solar system. A manned spacecraft has to take a suitable atmosphere with it; we have done this for the moon and perhaps we can do it even for Mars, but certainly not for the enormous distances and times that would be required to reach a planet attached to a nearby star. "Nearby" is a relative term. To reach a planet orbiting Alpha Centauri or Tau Ceti, two of the nearest stars, would take light, traveling at approximately 186,000 miles per second, a million years.

We will have to learn how to make space travel outside the solar system a possibility. We do not have the technology now, but perhaps some day we may. After what we have done already I would hesitate to say that it could never come to pass. Who would have been rash enough to predict fifty years ago that we would land a man on the moon and get him back to earth safely a couple of days later?

In the other direction there seems little that can be taken seriously. It has been claimed that some relics and monuments on the earth left over from previous civilizations can be interpreted to mean that the earth has from time to time been visited by creatures from other worlds. Unidentified flying objects (UFOs), drawings on buildings and carvings on hillsides have been read as signs of visitors from outer space, but I do not know of any serious scientists who accept the evidence. It seems more like wishful thinking than hard fact, and probably can be classified along with astrology as fanciful speculation.

The End of Life on Earth

According to the astronomers, who have made careful calculations based on what they have learned of other stars and planets, in about six billion years our sun will suddenly expand into what is called a red giant. It will become so hot and so large that it will at first evaporate all water on the earth and finally expand to absorb the planets altogether. That will mean of course not only the end of human life on the earth but also the end of the earth. Even if the earth remained after the sun became a red giant, it would leave nothing more than a burnt-out cinder, no place in which to live and maintain a civilization, for the sun itself would have shrunk to the size of what is called a white dwarf star, one too cool to provide the energy we need.

Does that mean the end of man and his civilizations? At first glance an event which is at least six billion years off is no cause for worry. But those who love mankind are not willing to face the prospect of the end of human life, however remote it may be. Therefore astronomers are even now speculating on the prospect of developing the technique necessary to establish colonies in space where they would be safe from annihilation by a dying sun. At first the experiment would be to establish a space colony at a point in space where the gravitational fields of the earth and of the moon exactly balance one another and where consequently a space station could remain. Then if this experiment proved successful the next effort would be to move the space colonies outside the solar system altogether and to where they would be able to develop with perfect security. Perhaps the best choice would be a planet which is revolving around some distant star whose prospects look more promising than those of our sun because the star is younger and thus could provide favorable conditions much longer.

There have been other and even more ambitious projects suggested, such as dismantling an unused planet, like Jupiter, which contains as much material as 38 earths, and reassembling some of it in usable form; or bombing Mercury, which is too hot anyway, in order to launch it into Jupiter's orbit, where it can be broken up and formed into a mini-sphere around that planet.

At least two physicists, Freeman Dyson and Adrian Berry,

think that we have the necessary technology to accomplish these feats. That such projects have been seriously proposed and not considered science fiction is at least significant.

It is time now to return, so to speak, to earth, and to consider some of the practical problems involved in such an ambitious set of projects as founding human colonies elsewhere in space. The first of these problems is the cost. The expense involved in landing a man on the moon and getting him back safely is enormous but has been borne. It must be remembered, however, that this large part of our national budget was spent in this way quite cheerfully because we were in competition with the Soviet Union. We won the race to the moon, and in terms of international prestige that was worth whatever it cost. But would we be willing to spend the additional millions of dollars it would take to establish even a modest colony in space? I doubt it. Not now, anyway. The budget of the space program has already begun to shrink considerably, and the vogue has declined. But the exploration of space is so new that we are not yet used to it. Military considerations are keeping it alive even if at a somewhat reduced pace, so there is always the hope that it may be expanded.

Already our horizons have been enlarged and the effects on our thoughts, feelings and actions affected correspondingly. Space exploration will undoubtedly be considered the greatest achievement of Western Civilization. Its consequences are even yet impossible to estimate correctly. Meanwhile the prospect of discovering—or establishing—civilizations in space remains the most exciting thing in the future, at least so far as we can see into it at the present time.

The Ideal Civilization

The thought that there must be millions of planets scattered throughout the vastness of space, and that on some of these planets there are, to repeat, civilizations less developed than ours while on others there are civilizations much more advanced, is nothing less than staggering. If we could only know something about the more advanced civilizations it might tell us the direction in which we shall be heading for the next few hundred thousand years.

Alas, at the present time the distances are too great and our technology, for all the miracles it has performed, is too feeble. We may learn to accelerate the speed of manned space ships until it approximates the speed of light. Contrariwise, the creatures on other planets where civilization is may be more advanced may learn how to visit us. Until one of these eventualities becomes a reality, however, we are compelled to fall back upon what civilizations we have had and what we have now.

Presumably, an ideal civilization would be one in which individuals would be at their happiest. No one would interfere with the happiness of others. There would be a government which was facilitative merely and not coercive. No wars, only peace; no conflicts, only co-operation; no competition, except of the friendliest sort.

It is easy to stitch together an ideal of this kind from the pieces we have, but would that be enough? Presumably not, unless it were to provide for further improvement. Evolution has taught us that as the human animal becomes more complex, his works and their effects on him grow more powerful, more intense. No primitive culture ever produced a Bach or a Shakespeare. What more complex and hence more powerful aesthetic qualities may lie in the future of the society of super-men who will inhabit the earth when they have developed out of the potentialities now dormant in us?

Faced with such speculations our imagination fails. We do not have the necessary philosophical tools to predict all the possibilities, still less are we equipped to separate out from all that there could be what it is preferable there should be.

It is impossible to foresee what lies ahead; if on a pessimistic note, this book closes also on a moral lesson: the more darkness the future casts across our path, the more we need each other and the less we can afford to add to the burdens we already carry. The terrible fact that individual life does not last forever but is to the contrary short and filled with natural ills, should be enough to warn us that life is all of a piece and no less so because each of us shares it.

Further Reading

Chapter 1

Linton, Ralph (ed.), *The Science of Man in The World Crisis* (New York 1945, Columbia University Press).

White, John, *A Voyage to Cochin China* (London 1972, Oxford University Press).

Chapter 2

Childe, V. Gordon, *Man Makes Himself* (New York 1951, New American Library).

———, *What Happens in History* (Baltimore 1952, Penguin).

Clark, Grahame, *World Prehistory* 2nd ed. (Cambridge 1969, University Press).

Coles, J. M., and Higgs, E. S., *The Archaeology of Early Man* (London 1969, Faber and Faber).

Hawkes, Jacquetta, *The First Great Civilizations* (New York 1973, Knopf).

———, and Woolley, Sir Leonard, *Prehistory and The Beginnings of Civilization* (New York 1963, Harper and Row).

Lee, R. B., and DeVore, I., (eds.), *Kalahari Hunter-Gatherers* (Cambridge, Mass., in press, Harvard University Press). Cf. also *Science*, 185, 932-934, 1974. The name of these hunters is spelled "!Kung". The exclamation point indicates a click at the beginning of the word, made by drawing the tongue sharply away from the roof of the mouth.

Renfrew, Colin, *Before Civilization* (New York 1973, Knopf).

Chapter 3

Hamilton, E., and Cairns, H., (eds.), *The Collected Dialogues of Plato* (New York 1961, Pantheon Books).
The Old Testament: The Book of Daniel
Sinclair, T. A., *Hesiod, Works and Days* (London 1932, Routledge).

Chapter 4

St. Augustine, *The City of God* (New York 1952, Modern Library).
For Orosius, see the account in Henry Osborn Taylor, *The Mediaeval Mind* 2 vols., vol. I, pp. 82-4, (London 1927, Macmillan).

Chapter 5

Khaldûn, Ibn, *The Muqaddimah*, translated by Franz Rosenthal. 3 vols. (New York 1958, Pantheon Books).
(There is an abridgment of the above work by N. J. Danwood. (Princeton, New Jersey 1967, University Press). There is also a longish review-essay of the Rosenthal translation by A. J. Liebling in *The New Yorker* for November 7, 1958.

Mahdi, Muhsin, *Ibn Khaldûn's Philosophy of History* (London 1957, George Allen and Unwin).

Rosenthal, Erwin I. J., *Political Thought in Medieval Islam* (Cambridge 1958, University Press. Chapter IV).

Chapter 6

Adams, H. P., *The Life and Writings of Giambattista Vico* (London 1935, Allen & Unwin).

Bergin, T. G., and Fisch, M. H., trans. *The New Science of Giambattista Vico* (Ithaca, New York 1948, Cornell University Press). All the quotations from Vico were taken from this translation.

————, trans. *The Autobiography of G. Vico* (Ithaca, New York 1944, Cornell University Press).

Chapter 7

Faure, Elie, *Napoleon* J. E. Jeffrey, trans. (New York 1925, Knopf). All of the quotations from Napoleon were taken from this translation.

Hegel, G. W. F., *The Philosophy of History*. J. Sibree, trans. (New York 1944, Willey).

Chapter 8

Marx, K., and Engels, F., *Basic Writings on Politics and Philosophy* L. S. Feuer, ed. (New York 1969, Doubleday).

Marx, K., and Engels, F., *Selected Works of Marx and Engels* (New York 1967, International Publishing Co.).

Chapter 9

There is no English translation of Danilevsky's work.

There is a German translation of *Russia And Europe: Russland Und Europa*, Notzel, Karl, trans. (Stuttgart and Berlin 1920).

There are good secondary accounts in Sorokin, Pitirim A., *Social Philosophies in An Age of Crisis* (Boston 1950, Beacon Press); Cairns, Grace, *Philosophies of History* (London 1962, Peter Owen).

Chapter 10

Hughes, H. Stuart, *Oswald Spengler* (New York 1952, Scribner).

Spengler, Oswald, *The Decline of The West* translated by C. F. Atkinson (New York 1945, Knopf).

Chapter 11

Toynbee, Arnold J., *A Study of History* 10 vols. (London 1934-1961, Oxford University Press).

——, *A Study of History*. Abridged Edition by D. C. Somervell. 2 vols. (London 1946-1957, Oxford University Press).

Chapter 12

Cairns, Grace, *Philosophies of History* (London 1962, Peter Owen).

Feibleman, James K., *The Theory of Human Culture* (New York 1968, Humanities Press).

Sorokin, Pitirim A., *Social Philosophies of An Age of Crisis* (Boston 1950, Beacon Press).

Chapter 13

Bordewich, Fergus M., "The Remains of British India" in *The New York Times* for April 28, 1974, Section 10, p. 1.

Murdock, George Peter, "The Common Denominator of Cultures" in Ralph Linton (ed.), *The Science of Man in the World Crisis* (New York 1945, Columbia University Press), pp. 123-142.

Chapter 14

Berry, Adrian, *The Next Ten Thousand Years: A Vision's of Man's Future in the Universe* (London 1974, Cape).

Brandt, John C., and Maran, Stephen P., *New Horizons in Astronomy* (San Francisco 1972, W. H. Freeman).

Jastrow, Robert, *Red Giants and White Dwarfs* (New York 1967, Harper and Row).
"Proposal for Human Colonies in Space", in *The New York Times* for May 13, 1974, page 1.

Sagan, Carl, (ed.), *Communication With Extraterrestrial Intelligence* (Cambridge, Mass., 1973, M.I.T. Press).

_____, *The Cosmic Connection* (New York 1973, Doubleday).

Index

229

DATE DUE

OC 5 '80			
OC 21 '80			
NO 1 1 '80			
AP 27 '83			
GAYLORD			PRINTED IN U.S.A.